WHAT READERS ARE SAYING ABOUT
"WISDOM BRINGS SUCCESS!"

*"**What an amazing gift for anyone who would choose to spare themselves from potentially totally avoidable mistakes** that could bring trouble for* years. The practical application of the scriptures and the very real, home-hitting stories that Dr. Brendan Kirby shares will turn your life around and set you on course for the very best God has in store for you. May the Holy Spirit speak and teach us all through this life changing book."

Dr. Jerry Stott, Global Associate Director (South Pacific), Foursquare Ministry International (FMI).

*"**Dr. Brendan has written one of the best books on wisdom that I have ever read.** His remarkable ability to integrate his extensive scientific background, including references to world-class researchers, with personal stories and lived pastoral experience, is incredibly helpful. Brendan skilfully handles the scriptures and presents everything in a logical and coherent manner, aided by helpful diagrams. This book is truly outstanding."*

Dr Richard Green, C3 Reach Regional Director; Founding Pastor and Senior Minister C3 Church Ryde.

*"**I think that it is excellent, and I love the personal stories and their application.** It is full of wisdom and will be a help to believers and pastors for an understanding of God's wisdom and how to live in it and avoid deception. The personal stories are windows that let the light of understanding in. I highly recommend this book."*

Dr Barry Manuel, Co-Pastor Healinglife Church Adelaide.

*"**Brendan shows where wisdom is, how to access it – but also its high challenges and rich rewards.** And it is filled with personal and real-life illustrations to make it's points clear. The section on finding wisdom in a culture of half-truths and lies is a manual for serious Christians. Use this study to develop moral muscle, the disciplines for character and the secret of knowing the Source of all Wisdom, in guiding your daily steps."*

Rev Ian Clarkson, Chairman, Hopenet SA Inc, Founder of Branches Church, Adelaide. Generate Foundational Standing Committee.

"The book 'Wisdom Brings Success' is certainly God–inspired; no one who reads can deny God's breadth and wisdom in it. So much is packed into the volume that could compel one seeking godly wisdom to keep coming back to tap from it from time to time. Of great interest and utmost importance ... is the discourse on "Why do we believe in a Creator?" and Prof Behe's DNA analysis proving God as the wise Designer which is impossible to counter–argue even by the hardest critics or atheists! ... Thanks Ps Brendan for this beautiful piece of work."

Pastor Jane and Abraham Haastrup, Assistant General Overseer,
and Pastor in charge of the Australia & Pacific Region, RCCG.

"Dr Brendan Kirby has written another useful book marrying both scripture and pragmatism. I have known Brendan for more than 30 years and he loves God's Word and to teach it accurately. He also holds a doctorate in physics and his good mind enables him to think through practical issues in life. Brendan is also an active pastor. All these factors make him well qualified to write a book on how biblical wisdom can help us to live life on this earth."

Pastor James Loke, Regional Pastor (Asia 4,6,7),
Hope International Ministries (HIM).

"I have found this book, written and compiled by Brendan, to be both helpful and challenging in relation to not only discovering wisdom, but living in wisdom, and seeking to avoid the many and varied traps of deception; whether from human sources or from the "deceiver" of our souls. ... I recommend this book to any industrious, serious student of the Word."

Ps Ken Graham; Founder pastor of Tea Tree Gully Community Church.

Prov 1: 5 A wise man will hear and increase learning, and a man of understanding will attain wise counsel

WISDOM
BRINGS SUCCESS

Knowing what is best, when it is not,
and discerning the difference when it matters!

Eccl 10:10
If the ax is dull and one does not sharpen
the edge, then he must use more
strength; but wisdom brings success.

DR BRENDAN J KIRBY

WESTBOW
PRESS®
A DIVISION OF THOMAS NELSON
& ZONDERVAN

WestBow Press books may be ordered through booksellers or by contacting:

WestBow Press
A Division of Thomas Nelson & Zondervan
1663 Liberty Drive
Bloomington, IN 47403
www.westbowpress.com
844-714-3454

ISBN: 979-8-3850-0948-0 (sc)
ISBN: 979-8-3850-0949-7 (e)

Library of Congress Control Number: 2023919172

Print information available on the last page.

WestBow Press rev. date: 1/15/2024

ABOUT THE AUTHOR

Married to Helen Kirby for over 29 years. BSc (Hons) 1983; PhD Physics, the University of Melbourne, 1989. Cofounding pastor with his wife Helen, of Hope Church in Klemzig, Adelaide in 1998. A member of the Australian National Executive of Hope International Ministries (HIM). Brendan assists Ps. Wilson Lim in overseeing a few hundred churches in Africa and India. Worked as a research scientist with 23 years' experience at three government research organizations: CSIRO Division of Wool Technology (Geelong), The Physics Department, Monash University (Melbourne) and DSTO Land Operations Division (Adelaide).

As part of a church planting movement (HIM), we have a vision to preach the gospel of eternal life to all those who believe in the Lord Jesus Christ and to make disciples and train leaders to plant churches all over the world (www.byhim.org).

PREVIOUS BOOK BY THE AUTHOR:

"*Your Faith Determines Your Future*" Lifting the Limits off your life.

Published by Westbow Press Books (2021).

HOPE CHURCH

53 Fourth Avenue, Klemzig, Adelaide, SA 5070, Australia.
Webpage: www.hopeadelaide.com
YouTube Channel: @hopechurchadelaide
Email: info@hopeadelaide.com
Twitter: @drbrendankirby

MISSIONS SUPPORT INFORMATION

All royalties from book sales shall be sent directly to pastors in India and Africa. If you would like to make a donation, see bank details below.

Account Name: Hope Missions Account
Account #118 373 340
BSB #105 056
SWIFT/BIC CODE for overseas transfers: SGBLAU2S
For USA transfers: Routing # 021 000 021
Bank SA, 87 John St, Salisbury, SA 5108, Australia.

Eccl 7:12b the excellence of knowledge is that wisdom gives life to those who have it.

Contents

Preface
WISDOM BRINGS SUCCESS!

Prov 4:5–8 "Get wisdom! Get understanding! Do not forget, nor turn away from the words of my mouth. Do not forsake her, and she will preserve you; love her, and she will keep you. Wisdom is the principal thing; therefore get wisdom.

I spoke to a couple intending to marry around 2003, and unfortunately I had the conviction to tell them that I did not think the marriage would go well. This was very unusual for me – probably only one of the rare times I've ever done so. This would be the man's first marriage but the lady's 3rd or 4th marriage, so I did not think that it had a strong enough character base. They got married and moved interstate and I did not hear from them again until about 10 years later when the man came to me and said "I should have listened to you. We are getting divorced." I was really sorry to hear that.

Life consists of results from the decisions we make. Not so much from what we are given, but of what we choose to do with what we are given. These choices are volitional, conscious decisions. These decisions form our character and our life. Decisions made under pressure can forge a heart of integrity and perseverance.

Wise decision making needs to be at the heart of our modus operandi (habitual way of operating). Everyone who has responsibility over others' lives should try their utmost to make wise decisions not only for themselves but for those for whom they influence and oversee.

The scripture exhorts us to seek wisdom (Job 28:20; Prov 8:17; Prov 19:8). The purpose of this book is to outline what wisdom is and its components, how to increase in wisdom and highlight why wisdom is precious and important. Foolishness in an age of compromise, complacency, and pragmatism is to be avoided at all costs.

We can all be wise (Prov 1:20; James 1:5). But foolishness is not just about making mistakes that could have been rectified with policies, procedures, a more systematic approach or a better fail-safe security system. Neither is wisdom just about being less emotional or smarter than others. In this book we want to take you on a journey which will hopefully improve your outlook on how to live a successful and wise life.

In this world it is impossible not to encounter and relate to deceitful people. It is incumbent upon us to learn how deception operates, its consequences, how it gains entry points into our lives, and how we can avoid and overcome deception.

I pray that you will persevere in reading this book to the end where we discuss the influence and effects of deception in our lives and how these affect our decision making.

Love Brendan J Kirby

Eccl 7: 19 Wisdom strengthens the wise more than ten rulers of the city.

Introduction

Prov 9:10 "The fear of the Lord is the beginning of wisdom, and the knowledge of the Holy One is understanding."

The laboratory door closed automatically behind me. At the time I was working for a division of the Australian government commonwealth scientific industrial research organization (CSIRO) in Geelong – a provincial city over 100km from family, friends and my church in Melbourne. There were no watchful eyes keeping me accountable for my behavior in this place. I was after some purified or deionized water for an experiment we were conducting at the time. As I entered the room I noticed concurrently that there was an attractive blonde experimental scientist in the room whom I knew from around the site, and also that there were no windows in the room. I asked her where the deionized water was so I could fill my small dispenser. She told me where it was and then said, "Let's have sex!" This sort of shocked me for a second, but I just shrugged it off thinking to myself, "You overstepped the line this time devil". I calmly remarked to the expectant woman, "This water is really good quality", not wanting to embarrass her; and then left the room. I saw the same woman walking around the site some days later and she looked noticeably deflated.

What has overcoming temptation got to do with wisdom? The fear of the Lord is the beginning of wisdom (Psalm 111:10; Prov 1:7; Prov 4:7) which encompasses turning away from evil. Wisdom is not always cognitive or logical, it has an indispensable spiritual component connected with our walk with the Lord (1Cor 2:7,10). At that time I did not realize that my turning away from secret sin was not just overcoming temptation, but also building a platform for a developing wisdom from God.

Wisdom comes from God, therefore walking with God is paramount in order to grow in wisdom (Amos 3:3). We cannot walk with God if we harbor secret sin; consequently the fear of the Lord (which restrains from wickedness) is the beginning of the foundation of a wise life.

Wisdom often employs knowledge, reason and logic in order to bring about a successful result (2Cor 1:17). Whereas foolishness often discards the restraint of self-control, neglects the pursuit of reason and knowledge, and often stumbles into various types of deception (e.g. Balaam, 2Pet 2:15, 16).

Prov 3:15 "She is more precious than rubies, and all the things you may desire cannot compare with her."

PART 1

WHAT IS WISDOM?

A tool that takes skill to use

James 3: 17 But the wisdom that is from above is first pure, then peaceable, gentle, willing to yield, full of mercy and good fruits, without partiality and without hypocrisy.

Wisdom is gentle, and a gentle answer turns away anger – whereas a harsh word stirs up strife (Prov 15:1). I was in Altona, Melbourne, (late 1980's) laughing with my mentor at the time, Dave Bernard, in my 1970 R10 Renault parked by the side of the road one Sunday afternoon after church. A young man full of tattoos (this is before they were commonplace) began to make a direct line to me from across the street. My driver's window was wound down so this young man walked up to my car and put both his elbows inside my car door window and began to push his face in towards mine, breathing out these words in a most threatening and provocative manner, "What are you laughing about?"

I sized up the situation instantly: a very rough street wise man with earrings and tattoos on his face and some of his teeth left, clearly used to intense violence, was challenging a passive university student inexperienced in physical confrontations. I calmly looked at him with respect, I tried very hard not to show any fear, and replied, "Oh sorry, we were just laughing about something my friend had just said. No harm intended." Instantly the angry young man who was ready to rip me out of the car changed facial expression to almost a smile, and said, "No problem. Have a good day!" My friend Dave turned to me, looking shocked and relieved exclaiming, "How on earth did you get out of that?? That was amazing!"

Learning and practicing to keep calm under pressure has kept me from taking unwise actions or making rash decisions. Since my teenage years I would practice keeping calm and cool – and tried hard not to allow stress to get to me. Again – little did I know that practicing such peaceful responses would also help provide a platform for developing wisdom.

Prov 14:29 Whoever is slow to anger has great understanding.

SECTION A: HOW DO WE RECOGNISE WISDOM?

James 3:13 Who is wise and understanding among you? Let him show by good conduct that his works are done in the meekness of wisdom.

Wisdom (dictionary): is the utilization and practical application of knowledge and experience, situations and people to bring about an optimum result and/or achievement concerning a group of people; wisdom is not IQ or intelligence.

Wisdom is a tool that takes skill to use: From the above definition we see that wisdom is a tool that utilizes resources (knowledge, experience, situations, people) to achieve a goal (optimal for the person utilizing the tool). If it's a tool then this means that 'wisdom' takes practice and skill to use and can be used for good or evil.

We choose to believe a particular worldview: The goals that people choose to pursue and their vision that they live for are governed by their worldview.

If we choose to follow the tenets of evolutionary ideas, then as Richard Dawkins stated years ago, "The universe we observe has precisely the properties we should expect if there is, at bottom, *no design, no purpose, no evil, no good, nothing but blind, pitiless indifference*"[1]. This worldview then sets up a set of values for individuals that are arbitrary and outside the reach of justice, ethics or morality. Even good deeds can be done because we want to do them rather than having them stem from a knowledge of right and wrong. Individuals apply wisdom in making decisions according to a materialistic, atheistic worldview in order to achieve their goals. This is what we refer to as "worldly wisdom".

The alternative form of wisdom is referred to as "godly wisdom" and is founded upon the logical and reasonable appraisal of the origin of both the universe and of life, and concludes that such complexity and wonder could only be designed and created. Random chance has no architecture or blueprint driving the formation of highly complex structures.

Why do we believe in a Creator? We infer design of a system if it exhibits the suitable criteria of irreducible complexity, as discussed cogently by Professor Behe[2]. Behe outlines various biological systems that require many proteins and enzymes to function and Behe classifies them as irreducibly complex. He provides a number of examples exhibiting such complexity that could conceivably only come from a Designer with a superior power and intelligence. Random mechanisms and statistical mechanics struggle to explain their origin. Behe makes this challenge specifically of the current secular wisdom regarding the origin of the human blood-clotting cascade which has over 50 interdependent proteins and enzymes interacting in a highly complex manner, acting autonomously with life and death at stake.

If we just look simplistically at our own human body (not considering the biochemical complexity at this stage): the engineering problem of distributing oxygen to over 30 trillion different sites (number of cells in

---

[1] Richard Dawkins, "*River out of Eden: a Darwinian view of life*", (1995) Basic Books (AZ).
[2] Michael J. Behe, "*Darwin's Black Box: The Biochemical Challenge To Evolution*", (1998) Simon & Schuster.

the human body) within 5 minutes on a continual 24/7 basis is mind-boggling. Various factors such as knowing what oxygen is and that we desperately need it to survive, detecting that it is in the atmosphere around us and developing a mechanism to ingest it can be taken for granted.

The construction of 100,000 km of tubing (arterial and venous channels), the design of a specific protein called haemoglobin that binds the oxygen molecule (how did our lungs know that oxygen is a gas molecule?) which then releases it to each cell for its metabolic requirements, the system for removing waste products (CO_2), and a pump (the heart) that does not stop for an average of 80 years (without a "battery" to power it) are all simply miraculous. Random chance and mutations struggle to explain blood-clotting[3] let alone the system of oxygen supply to the entire human body. (Remember that the description for these systems were all encoded in the beginning within a single cell's DNA).

Actually if we back-step for a moment, and consider even the random formation of a single protein – of which Mann states that there are between 80,000 and 400,000 in the human body[4]. These proteins are made up of 20 amino acids that all need to have a left-handed morphology, a particular type of bond, and a specific location for each amino acid within the protein chain. The probability of randomly assembling a typical protein with 150 amino acids is infinitesimal as calculated by Barnett[5], not to mention the random formation of haemoglobin as calculated by Blume[6].

King Solomon's pursuit of wisdom in the book of Ecclesiastes led to the final conclusion:

---

[3] Michael J. Behe, "*Darwin's Black Box: The Biochemical Challenge To Evolution*", (1998) Simon & Schuster.

[4] Matthias Mann; "*The Protein Puzzle*" Max Plank Research 3 (2017) page 3, https://www.mpg.de/11447927/MPR_2017_3.pdf

[5] Tim Barnett, "*Building A Protein By Chance*" (2015) https://www.str.org/w/building-a-protein-by-chance

[6] Stephen T.Blume, "*Do Richard Dawkins and Hemoglobin Destroy Evolution?*" (2013) https://evoillusion.org/3091-2/

Eccl 12:13,14 Let us hear the conclusion of the whole matter: *Fear God and keep His commandments*, for this is man's all. [14] For God will bring every work into judgment, including every secret thing, whether good or evil.

Therefore, it is wise to believe in a sovereign Creator God, and to make faith in God a rational foundation of our lives. This is an important building block in our journey of understanding wisdom.

How Does Wisdom Work?

In Chart 1 below is an outline of how wisdom and faith in God are connected. The bible states, *Psalm 14:1 "The fool has said in his heart, "There is no God."* The first stage of foolishness is to reject God.

Therefore, the first step of wisdom is to acknowledge that the glory of this whole creation – including the human body which is a biological and engineering marvel – has a Creator, who has revealed Himself through the Lord Jesus Christ (John 10:30, 36, 38; John 14:9) as prophesied hundreds of years previously (Psalm 16:10; Isaiah 7:14; 9:6; Psalm 22; Isaiah 53).

Since no One else has prophesied and fulfilled their own death and subsequent resurrection after 3 days (Matt 16:21; Matt 28:6), we can affirm that Jesus Christ is the unique Son of God who has provided the free gift of eternal life through His own death on the cross for us (Rom 5:15 – 18). It would be unwise to reject the offer of such a precious gift (Heb 2:3; 10:29).

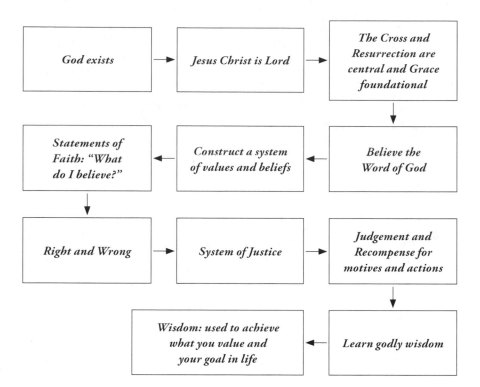

Chart 1: The beginning of the application of godly wisdom is to have faith in God, in Jesus Christ and the Word of God. This chart shows the sequence of our commitments and decisions: We understand that God exists, that Jesus Christ is the Son of God and that His sacrifice on the cross is pivotal for our salvation – these convictions are based upon a belief in the biblical record, from which we construct a set of values and faith statements by which we live by. The selection of what is right and wrong is predicated upon these values and beliefs. (As values and beliefs are altered by a society, their laws – right and wrong – are also modified.) Therefore a system of justice and recompense arises from our chosen worldview. This provides us with a foundation from which we learn godly wisdom and apply it to our lives.

We select a commensurate consistent set of values for our chosen worldview: With such a foundation we move on to believing and adhering to the Word of God from which we derive the values we live by. These values form the basis of our entire decision making. This system of values is very important and needs to be scrutinized regularly if we are to iteratively decrease the difference between what we say we believe and the values we actually live by. Our level of integrity is how well our "current values" (what we actually say and do) match with our "chosen values" (what we purport to value).

What do I value most in life?

WORLDLY VALUES	WORLDLY FRUIT
Beauty	Pride
Talent	Rejection
IQ	Insecurity
Strength	Jealousy
Body Shape	Selfish ambition
Prominence/ Fame	Competition
Fortune	Comparison

Figure 1a Worldly values and their fruit

What do I value most in life?

GODLY VALUES	GODLY FRUIT
Character	Peace
Integrity	Love
Honesty	Joy
Effort/ Hard work	Self-acceptance
Perseverance	Self-Control
Purity	Faithful
Obedience	Kindness

Figure 1b Godly values and their fruit

These two figures indicate the contrasting fruit in our lives resulting from the choices we previously made regarding what we have chosen to value. Unfortunately some people choose their values by osmosis (family or peer influence) rather than by a cognitive rational process of what is truly valuable in an eternal context.

These values give us a system of justice to provide structure to a civilized Christian society and provide a set of recompenses for law breakers. Without a coherent set of unchanging values to undergird society with and to provide guidance for all behaviors, we as a people are left bereft of a firm foundation and are left to the whims of moral winds which blow us in various directions. Wisdom must have such a coherent set of values informing its decision making.

In Figures 1a and 1b above we propose certain values that follow the choice of either a worldly or godly worldview. Then we align these values with the "fruit" or consequences (evidence) of each value. For example, if we value "*Beauty*" then the worldly fruit of "*Pride*" may well ensue.

Jesus Christ taught us that we "will know them by their fruits" (Matt 7:16, 17, 20). For example, the fruit of jealousy can be the result of the worldly values of exalting body shape and beauty.

Wisdom Takes Skill and Practice

Wisdom is a tool that is used to accomplish the vision for our lives. The vision we choose to live for is determined by what we believe and therefore what we value. If we choose worldly self-centered values then we can apply the same framework of wisdom as discussed below to achieve our selfish vision.

In their erudite commentary on the book of proverbs in the ESV Study Bible, Garrett and Harris[7] discuss the different types of character revealed through the proverbs: the wise, the fool, the simple, the scoffer and those wise in their own eyes. The wise have learned the "skill of living out the covenant" of God in everyday situations, or "skill in the art of godly living". The fool is "steadily opposed to God's covenant" and can be a dangerous person. Garrett and Harris elucidate the simple as someone who is "not firmly committed either to wisdom or to folly", is easily misled, and "does not apply discipline" to their lives to become wise. They also comment that the "wise is seen from the perspective of his skill of living out God's will".

The Hebrew word for wisdom is *khokmah*, which can entail a component of skill in its meaning, "particularly the skill of choosing the right course of action for a desired result"[8].

---

[7] Duane A. Garrett, The Southern Baptist Theological Seminary, and Kenneth Laing Harris, Covenant Theological Seminary. *Commentary on the book of Proverbs*, The ESV Study Bible (2008), Published by Crossway, Wheaton, Illinois, USA.
[8] Garrett and Harris, *ibid*.

Job 38: 36 Who has put wisdom in the inward parts or given understanding to the mind?

SECTION B: WISDOM CAN BE CORRUPTED

The prophet Ezekiel refers to "the King of Tyre" (Ezek 28:12) as having been in the Garden of Eden, therefore we can infer that the subsequent references about this "King" are actually for Lucifer (Isaiah 14:12) rather than a human king. Ezekiel states that "you corrupted your wisdom":

Ezekiel 28:17 "Your heart was lifted up because of your beauty; you corrupted your wisdom for the sake of your splendor; I cast you to the ground, I laid you before kings, that they might gaze at you."

Lucifer became proud because of his beauty, and chose worldly values in order to exalt his own splendor. In Genesis 3:1 various versions refer to the serpent as cunning, crafty, shrewd or subtle. The words cunning and crafty both have an element of deceit, while subtle is defined as "making use of clever and indirect methods to achieve something". We could conclude that Lucifer corrupted his wisdom with deceit and cunning in order to pursue his selfish ambitions (Isaiah 14:13, 14).

Our spiritual enemy is wiser than any human being which should remind us never to underestimate the enemy's strategies, yet he is not wiser than the Lord of course (1Cor 2:7,8).

The Prince of Tyre used wisdom for worldly gain: The prophet Ezekiel was tasked by the Lord to deliver this word to the prince of Tyre who was a corrupt ruler:

Ezek 28:2b – 5 "Because your heart is lifted up, and you say, 'I am a god, I sit in the seat of gods, in the midst of the seas,' yet you are a man, and not a god, though you set your heart as the heart of a god [3] (Behold, you are wiser than Daniel! There is no secret that can be hidden from you! [4] With your wisdom and your understanding you have gained riches for yourself, and gathered gold and silver into your treasuries; [5] *by your great wisdom in trade you have increased your riches, and your heart is lifted up because of your riches) ...*"

With the above two cases in mind, it is possible to be wise and to be wicked. Therefore the wisdom that the wicked utilize is still a form of wisdom (*"you are wiser than Daniel!"* commends the scripture) but for worldly gain. Hence the classification of two types of wisdom: a worldly wisdom and a godly wisdom (1Cor 3:20). In this light – wisdom can be regarded as the skillful use of a "tool" by which either the godly or the wicked achieve their ends.

The apostle James clarifies this corruption of wisdom revealing the satanic spiritual influence:

James 3:14 – 16 But if you have bitter envy and self-seeking in your hearts, do not boast and lie against the truth. [15] *This wisdom does not descend from above, but is earthly, sensual, demonic.* [16] *For where envy and self-seeking exist, confusion and every evil thing are there.*

Of course the first contact with worldly wisdom was in the Garden of Eden and it appealed to Eve in order to make her wise:

Gen 3:6 So when the woman saw that the tree *was good for food*, that it *was pleasant to the eyes*, and a tree *desirable to make one wise*, she took of its fruit and ate. She also gave to her husband with her, and he ate.

God's intention is not to make us wise and become independent of Him, but for us to have a supernatural wisdom that refutes our accusers and those who oppose us. A wisdom that is based on a daily relationship with Him. God loves us and desires continual communion with us, not just to be a one-off wisdom dispenser.

Chart 1 finishes with the statement that *"Wisdom is used to achieve what you value and your goal in life"*. Alternatively, we could say that wisdom is a tool that is utilized to achieve progress according to the set of values we adopt.

Wisdom achieves the vision!

We need to consider our value system because each of us is building a house and our values determine what type of house we will build for ourselves and others. The "house" in this case if figurative for the vision of our lives – what we are building with our lives.

Prov 24:3, 4 Through wisdom a house is built, and by understanding it is established; ⁴by knowledge the rooms are filled with all precious and pleasant riches.

Wisdom leads to Success: *Eccl 8: 1 Who is like a wise man? And who knows the interpretation of a thing? A man's wisdom makes his face shine, and the sternness of his face is changed.*

Why does a wise man's face shine? Because he has the joy of success and victory in his life (Eccl 10:10). Wisdom will lead to the right decisions, correct relationship choices, financially viable investments, career progress, marital harmony and connection with The Almighty (2Cor 2:14)! The enemy of such wisdom is our own foolishness and neglect.

We need to be wise in order to:

Achieve our Goal and Vision – every person needs a motivating compelling vision.

Make the best decisions – weighing up different options (short term gain or long term pain).

Avoid making foolish mistakes – by learning from our own and others' past errors.

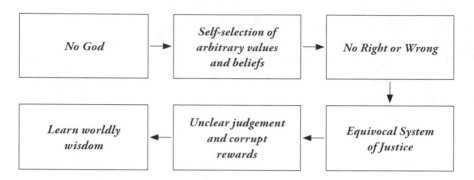

Chart 2: Reveals that rejecting a knowledge of God and choosing our own values ("stealing can be beneficial") leaves us with no foundation for right and wrong, and consequently with little structure to our system of justice. In this case the 'worldly wisdom' people use is to advance their own desires.

Job 28:12, 18, 20, 23, 28 "But where can wisdom be found? And where is the place of understanding? [18] For the price of wisdom is above rubies, [20] From where, then, does wisdom come? And where is the place of understanding? [23] God understands the way to it, and he knows its place. [28] And to man He said, 'Behold, the fear of the Lord, that is wisdom, and to depart from evil is understanding.' "

In Chart 2 above we look at the result of rejecting faith in God. It leads to a set of values that we can choose for ourselves and can change whenever we like. Ultimately there is no right or wrong, there are simply different consequences for our decisions and actions. Politicians and country leaders sometimes change their values to suit themselves or their people, and justice becomes corrupted because the values informing our legal system become relative.

Chart 2 describes another type of wisdom emerging through a divergent set of values – a set of values derived from ourselves rather than from divine origin. Worldly wisdom becomes the fog that clouds the clear skies of godly, divine wisdom.

CONCLUSION

God wants His people to reflect His wisdom. He desires us to succeed in every area of life utilizing His wisdom and direction for us. Jesus Christ sends us out on a Great Commission and commends us to be alert, to be wise, and to be innocent:

Matt 10: 16 "Behold, I send you out as sheep in the midst of wolves. Therefore be wise as serpents and harmless as doves."

Chapter Review

Wisdom is a tool that takes skill to use.

People choose to adopt a specific worldview: one based upon randomness and evolution or design and creation.

Then people select a commensurate consistent set of values that match their chosen worldview.

The values people live by flow from their worldview.

These values then form the basis of all of our decision making.

The level of the integrity of our decision making depends upon how well our "current values" (what we actually say and do) match with our "chosen values" (what we purport to value).

How do we Respond?

Have we decided which worldview best fits with the reality of the world around us?

Do we know what our values of life are?

Are our values based upon our own opinions and feelings and what our friends think, or are they chosen because of what we have come to believe about life?

Ps 111:10 The fear of the LORD is the beginning of wisdom; a good understanding have all those who do His commandments. His praise endures forever.

2

WHY IS WISDOM IMPORTANT?

Famous cases of foolishness and wisdom

Prov 24:3 – 6 Through wisdom a house is built, and by understanding it is established; ⁴ by knowledge the rooms are filled with all precious and pleasant riches. ⁵ A wise man is strong, yes, a man of knowledge increases strength; ⁶ for by wise counsel you will wage your own war, and in a multitude of counselors there is safety.

The above proverb describes some of the beauty of the fruit of godly wisdom – the house is built up, it is established (built upon the Rock), it also prospers with love and joy, produces strength and successful ventures.

I still have the scars of foolishness on my own face from over 40 years ago (7am, 12ᵗʰ Jan 1982 actually). I was rushing down the long Looker Road hill in Lower Plenty (Melbourne) on my bicycle at about 60km/ hr towards an intersection whose traffic lights were green. I was hoping to get to the station to catch a train so I could get to the Aeronautical Research Laboratories (ARL) early that day. I knew that the lights would change to red by the time I arrived at the intersection – but because I had a high speed I erroneously thought I could make it across the four lane intersection (with median strip) before the cars in the opposing direction accelerated. I woke up in hospital! I vaguely remembered going through the red light, and a picture of a car on my left hand side speeding towards me. I immediately checked my bones for fractures. I had gone head first into the bitumen road and been knocked unconscious. Miraculously I was unhurt and released from observation a few hours later. My face looked like it was a red tomato – but I was OK. How foolish was I to risk my life so I could catch the early train that day, so that I could earn a few more dollars that week. I was not yet 20 years old at the time – and almost didn't make it to my next birthday.

SECTION A: FOOLISHNESS IS VERY COSTLY

If wisdom is required to build a house full of good fruit such as love, joy, peace and self-control – then conversely it is easier to foolishly destroy something (knock it down) than to build it up.

Fool (dictionary): a person who acts unwisely or imprudently; rash courage or foolishly bold; lacking good sense or judgment.

Psalm 38:5 My wounds stink and fester because of my foolishness …

Wisdom on its own is sometimes not appreciated (2Sam 16:23). Wisdom really begins to achieve the recognition and appreciation that it deserves when placed in contrast with either foolish actions or unwise mistakes. Foolishness can be defined as not only "foolish actions" but also behavior that lacks foresight, a deficiency of forward planning or a rejection of sound wisdom. From a spontaneous comment that causes embarrassment, to an action that results in the discord and severance of long term relationships, to actual loss of life, foolish behavior is costly and damaging. Some examples of poor decision-making or mistakes with dire consequences that can be regarded as foolish in terms of lack of either attention to detail or foresight can be seen below:

The Avoidable Dam Collapse: On the 19th July 1985 the embankment of the upper basin (or small reservoir) of the Val Di Stava Dam collapsed onto the lower basin which in turn collapsed. Around 180,000 cubic metres of muddy mass made up of sand, silt and water descended downstream at the speed of almost 90 km per hour and swept away people, trees, and houses until it reached the confluence of the Rio Stava and Avisio streams[9]. Few of the people were able to survive. Along its path, the mudslide caused the death of 268 people and the complete destruction of many buildings and bridges[10]. This disaster could have been avoided by those managing the mines who could have repaired these tailings dams when needed prior to their collapse. Their motive was to make money rather than provide safer structures for the dams. The result of their values was a foolish decision to prevaricate (delay) which cost 268 lives and sent those responsible to jail for manslaughter.

Adhering to the foolish value of making of money above the safety of people's lives can lead to decisions that result in disastrous consequences.

The Sinking of The Titanic and a Missing Key: Prior to the Titanic setting sail, the second officer David Blair was replaced by Charles Lightoller. The cabinet that kept the binoculars for observing icebergs had been previously locked by Blair who left the ship unknowingly keeping the key to this cabinet in his pocket. Fred Fleet, who was in charge of sighting for icebergs, later stated to the senate enquiry that if he had had access to the binoculars then he "could have seen the impending disaster well in advance to prevent it". Who would have thought that one missing key could possibly be the cause of so much trouble[11].

---

[9] Val Di Stava Dam Collapse (1985), https://www.stava1985.it/il-crollo/
[10] Val Di Stava Dam Collapse (1985) https://en.wikipedia.org/wiki/Val_di_Stava_dam_collapse
[11] Ananta Sharma, "*7 Stupid Mistakes That Changed The Course Of History Drastically*", (2015) https://www.storypick.com/stupid-mistakes-made-history-weep/

The German Failure to Withstand the D-day Attack: Erwin Rommel, a highly esteemed and respected German military general, was placed in charge of the defense of the coast of France from littoral warfare. Rommel was regarded as a military genius and was a formidable opponent. Due to inclement weather in early June 1944, Rommel expected the landing by the allied forces along the coast of France to be deferred – so he took the day off to visit his wife on her birthday[12]. The weather cleared and Eisenhower gave the go-ahead to Operation Overlord, and the D-Day attack along the coast of Normandy began. The combination of Rommel being absent from the battlefield and Hitler's order not to disturb him while sleeping provided sufficient advantage to the Allies that they were able to gain a foothold along the coast. If the German tanks had been mobilized sooner, it may well have been a very different story[13].

The Mars Climate Orbiter Crash: On September 23, 1999, NASA lost contact with the Mars Climate Orbiter spacecraft, as it approached the red planet. The contracting company to NASA developed their software using imperial units and measures instead of the expected metric system of units[14]. This relatively simple oversight (compared with the complexity of the whole project) led to errors in the guidance of the spacecraft and its eventual demise as it crashed on the planet surface[15].

Foolish mistakes, like a hasty military operation, an opportunistic business venture or a cursory decision to marry – can be expensive and costly. The cost is measured in the scars on human hearts and lives.

---

[12] Ananta Sharma, *ibid.*

[13] Joseph V. Micallef (2019) *While Hitler Snored: D-Day, Rommel and the Panzers* https://www.military.com/daily-news/2019/05/31/while-hitler-snored-d-day-rommel-and-panzers.html and *A Bodyguard of Lies: How the Allies Deceived Germany about D-Day*, https://www.military.com/daily-news/2019/06/05/bodyguard-lies-how-allies-deceived-germany-about-d-day.html see also: Erwin Rommel, Normandy and Conspiracy, https://www.britannica.com/topic/Wehrmacht

[14] Ananta Sharma, *ibid.*

[15] Mars Climate Orbiter, NASA Science, https://solarsystem.nasa.gov/missions/mars-climate-orbiter/in-depth/ see also Siddiqi, Asif (2018) Beyond Earth: A Chronicle of Deep Space Exploration, p.1958-2016. NASA History Program Office, X.

The problem: As society we tend to care little about wisdom or reason. Foolishness despises wisdom and doesn't take care to think carefully or reasonably. Those who become foolish have little foresight, live for ephemeral goals, develop bad habits, and focus on their passions and desires. Some, as a consequence, experience split families, abuse, heartbreak or betrayal, and as a result become hurt, angry, distrusting, and resentful. Unfortunately they can still continue to pursue their own interests leading to further foolishness and deception.

Some people turn away from the knowledge of God because of the pain or trauma they experience. This is a great tragedy as the Lord wants to reach out and heal their pains and bruises. Broken lives, shattered dreams and torn relationships leave people bereft and lacking trust in others.

We cannot pursue the wisdom of God and the wisdom of this world at the same time (1Cor 1:20). There is a wisdom of the world which leads to selfish ambition, jealousy, the love of money, pride, lust, competition, hatred and bitterness.

There is a wisdom from God which leads to focusing on love, kindness and eternal things rather than the temporal. In the world's eyes, God's wisdom is foolish. In God's eyes, the wisdom of this world is foolish.

1Cor 3:19,20 For the wisdom of this world is foolishness with God. For it is written, "He catches the wise in their own craftiness"; [20] and again, "The Lord knows the thoughts of the wise, that they are futile."

The great tragedy is that few seek after godly wisdom. Our culture trains itself to pursue the feelings and impulses of our carnal nature and gratification of our own appetites – instead of pursuing meaning, self-control, significance, vision, and loving relationships. Achievement, ambition, feelings and impulses are taking precedence over love, reason, logic and wisdom.

We study and succeed academically, and diligently work hard but even with our human achievements, it is possible for us to still remain foolish: *Rom 1: 22 "Professing to be wise they became fools".*

It is foolish to invest everything into this world when we will die sometime in the future. It is wise to invest into the Kingdom of God because it is eternal. Nothing can surpass an eternal inheritance! Chart 3 below gives us a simple outline of applying godly wisdom:

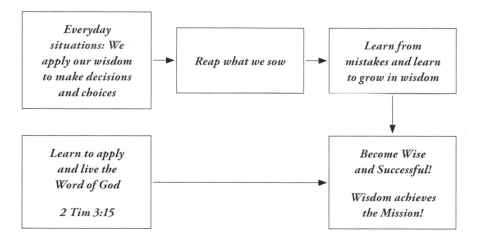

Chart 3: Process of applying godly wisdom in order to become successful

Wisdom is highly beneficial

One of the most famous applications of wisdom is when King Solomon had recently established his reign through decisive action in dealing with Joab, Shimei and Adonijah. Two prostitutes arguing over the ownership of one surviving baby came before the king and each claimed that the baby placed before them was their own. No other witnesses were present and it would be impossible to discern who was lying from simple observation. God had promised Solomon great wisdom of heart, and we begin to see it in action in this altercation between the two mothers: the King states "Bring me a sword … divide the living child in two" (1King 3:24, 25). One prostitute said callously "Divide him!" but the real mother cried out for the life of the child and pleaded that the King give the other woman the child. Discerning who the true mother was using wisdom advanced King Solomon's reputation considerably, for "the people knew the wisdom of God was in him to administer justice" (1King 3:28).

David was known to behave wisely in his military endeavours even while he was still supporting King Saul (1Sam 18:5, 14, 15, 30). I believe the secret to his exceptional wisdom at a young age was his dependence upon God's guidance – the scripture commends in the same chapter a few times that "the Lord is with him" (1Sam 18:12, 14, 28). This dependence upon the Lord led him into some great successes (1Sam 23:5), strategic evasive action (1Sam 23:13) and outright victory (1Sam 30:6; 2Sam 5:25). While David enquired of the Lord, he was always successful in his ventures. When he neglected to do so, then we see stress, tension, conflict and eventually insurrection (1Sam 27:1, 2Sam 11:1; 2Sam 15:14) coming into his life. His strength became his weakness through neglect. A good warning for us.

Ahithophel was so wise he was regarded almost as an oracle of God (2Sam 16:23) and he gave strategic evil wise advice to Absalom. Yet who was wiser, Hushai the Archite or Ahithophel? Hushai may not have had the spectacular military wisdom of Ahithophel, but he aligned himself with God's anointed prophet King David. Ahithophel foolishly aligned himself with Absalom hoping for some temporary gain for himself, but lost everything! Aligning ourselves with God and His people is always the wisest course of action (2Cor 12:18). It is astonishing how some highly intelligent and even very wise people can make patently foolish errors in judgement, as Ahithophel did. We see again that wisdom is a tool that can be used for either good or for evil.

Satan's original sin was most likely pride and selfish ambition (Isaiah 14:13, 14) and pride is self-deceiving (Gal 6:3). It is interesting that satan thought the crucifixion of the Son of God would be his moment of glory, and in no way anticipated it to be to his demise. This is a great example where the wisdom of God prevailed over satanic, worldly wisdom:

1Cor 2:6 – 8 However, we speak wisdom among those who are mature, yet not the wisdom of this age, nor of the rulers of this age, who are coming to nothing. ⁷ But we speak the wisdom of God in a mystery, the hidden wisdom which God ordained before the ages for our glory, ⁸ which none of the rulers of this age knew; for had they known, they would not have crucified the Lord of glory.

SECTION B: WISDOM AND THE POWER OF GOD

We need more of the wisdom of God in our lives to thwart the enemy's attacks against us. The apostle Paul actually does not want us to rely upon the worldly wisdom of men ("wisdom of this age"), but upon the power of God:

1 Cor 2:1 – 5 And I, brethren, when I came to you, did not come with excellence of speech or of wisdom declaring to you the testimony of God. ² For I determined not to know anything among you except Jesus Christ and Him crucified. ³ I was with you in weakness, in fear, and in much trembling. ⁴ And my speech and my preaching were not with persuasive words of human wisdom, but in demonstration of the Spirit and of power, ⁵ that your faith should not be in the wisdom of men but in the power of God.

Wisdom, God's Purpose and godly Values: Chart 4 below reminds us that godly wisdom will achieve success in our lives, with the proviso that we align ourselves with God's vision and God's purposes – lest we be found asking God to make us successful for our own sake only.

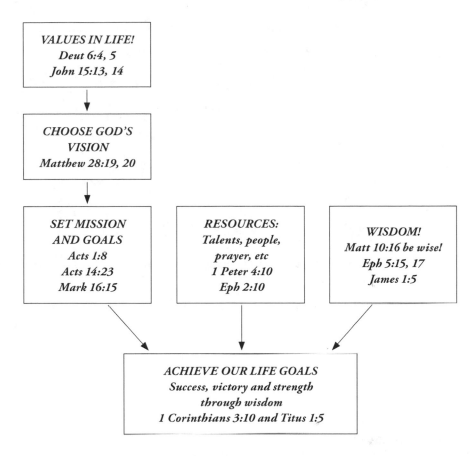

Chart 4: Process of applying wisdom in order to achieve our life goals. Here the achievement of our life goals has 3 inputs: our mission and goals (direction of activities), our available resources and our source of wisdom to guide us.

According to James, wisdom based on self-centred values, earthly or worldly wisdom will lead us astray:

James 3:14 – 16 But if you have bitter envy and self-seeking in your hearts, do not boast and lie against the truth. [15] This wisdom does not descend from above, but is earthly, sensual, demonic. [16] For where envy and self-seeking exist, confusion and every evil thing are there.

Wisdom based on God's values (pure, peaceful, gentle, submissive, merciful, loving, joyful, self-controlled, equity, integrity), is the wisdom that comes from above – or godly wisdom – and will always lead us into success! James lists 8 components of wisdom from heaven:

James 3:17 But the wisdom that is from above is first pure, then peaceable, gentle, willing to yield, full of mercy and good fruits, without partiality and without hypocrisy.

How can we use the phrase *"will always lead us into success"*? Because nothing can defeat the purposes of God (Isaiah 54:17, Rom 8:31, 37), and if we continually align our lives with His vision and purpose for us (2Tim 4:7,8) – then His plan for us will come to pass (Ps 138:8, Phil 1:6)!

As stated in Eccl 10:10 wisdom brings success, and this success is achieving God's design, calling and purpose for our lives, as King David did (Acts 13:36).

CONCLUSION

Nobody wants or plans to be foolish, but how many of us do or say foolish things at times when we are under pressure? Our goal is to be foolish less and less, and to be wiser more often. We can do it! We can all become more wise and grow in wisdom as a lifelong pursuit. Let us be determined to embark on a journey of increasing wisdom without turning back to foolishness and sin.

It is possible to achieve great things for the Lord. Wisdom is in the midst of many wise counsellors (Prov 15: 22). If we desire to do our best in life for the Lord, then we need to be wise by listening to the advice of others at times. Wisdom helps us to work hard and effectively to achieve our best. Foolishness walks with apathy and complacency.

James 1: 5 If any of you lacks wisdom, let him ask of God, who gives to all liberally and without reproach, and it will be given to him.

Chapter Review

We all need wisdom – as the cost of foolishness is measured in the scars on human hearts and lives.

Discuss the charts that flow from these choices of worldview and values.

What can be added to these charts to make them more comprehensive?

Wisdom is beneficial e.g.:

King Solomon's decision to give the baby to its actual mother in 2Kings 3;

King David's decision to circle behind the Philistine enemy in 2Sam 5;

Hushai the Archite's advice that thwarted the wisdom of Ahithophel, and

The wisdom of God that thwarted the rulers of this age (1Cor 2:8).

How do we Respond?

Recently I gave an altar call to a group of church leaders to respond to the need for wisdom to help them solve their problems. Only one responded. None of the pastors responded. What should our response be if someone asks if we need more wisdom?

How do we make the request and search for wisdom more of a continual lifestyle?

If we are in an area of responsibility then the decisions we make can critically affect others' lives. How can we have confidence before God that we are making the best decisions and giving the wisest advice?

Prov 11:29 He who troubles his own house will inherit the wind, and the fool will be servant to the wise of heart.

COMPONENTS OF WISDOM

A pictorial description

1Cor 1:22 – 24 For Jews request a sign, and Greeks seek after wisdom; but we preach Christ crucified, to the Jews a stumbling block and to the Greeks foolishness, ²⁴but to those who are called, both Jews and Greeks, Christ the power of God and the wisdom of God.

Wisdom and the power of God: I used to ride my bicycle on the roads quite a lot – especially before I bought my third hand, run down R10 (1970) Renault. I would have been perhaps 18 or 19 years of age, and was hurtling down a very long descent on Lower Plenty Road on my bicycle racing towards the intersection with Yallambie Road in the afternoon (the peak hour traffic had not yet begun). I must have been moving down this extended hill at over 60km per hour – which was fast for a young bike rider such as myself at the time. I noticed a car at the intersection that hadn't quite stopped. I was so confident that the car would stop because I was moving so fast that the car would have no time to fully pull out into Lower Plenty Road. I did not look up, but focused on the bitumen road below me. Perhaps a second or so passed, and I looked up again to check the approaching intersection for traffic, and I saw the car that "did not have time to pull out" had drifted instead out from Yallambie

Road into Lower Plenty Road. This meant his car was directly in front of me! I was about four meters away from the car.

As I looked up, I immediately assessed that because of my rapid speed of approach, that I had no chance of swerving to miss the vehicle suddenly in my way. Turning the bicycle's steering wheel at that speed would not have changed its direction – besides, I did not even have time to turn the steering wheel. My brain was calculating how my bike would impact just in front of the driver's door and how my body would be thrown into and across his car. A silent scream began to flow through my mind as I grasped this reality in front of me.

What seemed like a third of a second later, I noticed that my bicycle was passing in front of the car, well clear of the bumper bar. There was no swerving, no change of direction, it was as if I just continued on a straight line. My bicycle continued on effortlessly at speed for another 100m or so while I tried to breathe and regain some composure. I was shocked, perplexed, astonished and stunned. The driver seemed transfixed by what had just happened, as his car did not move away for seconds afterwards. I looked back angrily shaking my head at the driver!

(In retrospect I thought that perhaps the driver had not wanted to stop just for a cyclist, but soon realised he did not have enough time to accelerate his car fully out onto the road, so he had just stopped in his indecision in the middle of my lane!)

Afterwards, I began to realise how impossible it was for my bicycle to physically have changed its path with no movement on my part – I had not moved a muscle. I had not jerked my hands in evasive action. All I had time for was to see an inevitable crash. I had been on a direct line straight into the car. Then in less than half a second I was on a parallel line still going straight, but in front of the car. This was one spectacular occasion when God intervened in the course of my life – and perhaps saved my life. Ladies and gentlemen – we need the power of God in our lives to deliver us from impossible situations! Christ crucified is both the power of God and the wisdom of God, amen!

SECTION A: CAN WE SHOW THE
PROOF OF OUR WISDOM?

Prov 1:5 A wise man will hear and increase learning, and a man of understanding will attain wise counsel ...

Prov 9:9 Give instruction to a wise man, and he will be still wiser; teach a just man, and he will increase in learning.

A medical doctor asked me, "Are you wise?" with a tinge of disbelief in his tone. I said "yes" relatively confidently. Why? Because a wise man listens and learns. You do not need to be a genius to be wise. We can all be wise. Wisdom can then be vindicated by the quality of its decision making.

Jesus Christ said that *"wisdom is vindicated by her children"* (Matt 11:19 and Luke 7:5) as an answer to His accusers who were looking to merely find fault. So what are these "children" of wisdom that the Lord is referring to? Our wise actions or words will produce good fruit. People will know either our wisdom or our foolishness as they will be likewise evident by their fruit (Matt 7:16). Hence it is possible to prove that we are wise by the fruit of our decision making over the years.

In order to grow in wisdom we will need to self-assess our own fruit, and discuss with others, get feedback from our team – and be patently honest whether it was a foolish decision or a good one.

Paul the apostle challenges us to "show the proof of our love" (2Cor 8:24) while James challenges us to show the proof of our wisdom! He then succinctly delineates the fruit of worldly wisdom and godly wisdom.

James 3:13 Who is wise and understanding among you? Let him show by good conduct that his works are done in the meekness of wisdom.

A word of Wisdom

1Cor 12:7, 8 But the manifestation of the Spirit is given to each one for the profit of all: ⁸ for to one is given the word of wisdom through the Spirit, …

Sometimes a word of wisdom can turn a church or organisation from mediocrity to growth. It was around early November 2015 and Paul Joswig, Andy Leake and I were having a core team discussion in the Gilles Plains McDonalds after a prayer meeting. Helen (my wife of 21 years at that time) had decided she was too tired to attend another late night meeting. We discussed various matters, but the big one that night was whether the church should stay in a brand new, large council building with ample dedicated car parking, that was adjacent to a sports oval with parkland and children's playground, located on the main road where 1000's of cars drove past our church A-frame every day, whose rent cost us only $60 per Sunday? Or whether it should move to a recently rented, smaller building off a side street a couple of km away, in a very old shopping centre, with a run-down façade and a major parking problem during soccer season?

A recently conducted survey of the opinion of church members had been divided about 50/50 which did not assist in our decision making. Our collective wisdom at the end of a fruitful discussion was that we should stay where we were in the new council building on the main road. I rang Helen to inform her of our wonderful perspicacious decision. She instantly replied saying, "No! We should move. The Lord has shown me we should move to the older building!"

I couldn't believe it. How to contradict your husband (and pastor, I might add) in front of your team. I nervously said "Oh". The history behind my stalling was that I knew that when my wife used the phrase "The Lord has shown me …" I had better listen. I had been embarrassed too many times in the past when I hadn't listened! I thought to myself, "Oh. This is embarrassing and annoying!" Being a "wise leader" I found a solution to try and save my leadership reputation. "OK, let's move then!" The guys were shocked that I agreed so quickly with Helen in turning around a decision deliberated upon by more than an hour's "wise" team discussion. But my sagacious escape clause was, "Let's move for a few weeks, and see how it goes. If all goes well, great! If not, we can always move back." There was no need to wait even a few weeks. After the 2nd Sunday in the older venue the spirit in the church was so blessed and the people full of joy and the fellowship wonderful, that it was obviously God's choice to move. Humble pie again for the husband (and pastor)! For the next 6 years the church hardly stopped growing and God's blessings have continued to flow. We thank God for Helen's word of wisdom at that time, and we laugh at our own mistake!

This is a pertinent lesson for leaders, that wisdom is in a multitude of counsellors (Prov 15:22; 11:14).

Psalm 85:8 I will hear what God the Lord will speak, for He will speak peace to His people and to His saints; but let them not turn back to foolishness.

SECTION B: WHAT ARE THE DIFFERENT COMPONENTS OF GODLY WISDOM?

If we are to break down the different components of wisdom then we can begin with a rough idea for an architecture of wisdom – as the bible discusses 7 pillars of wisdom and that wisdom builds her house:

Prov 9:1 "Wisdom has built her house, she has hewn out her seven pillars".

Prov 24:3, 4 Through wisdom a house is built, and by understanding it is established; ⁴by knowledge the rooms are filled with all precious and pleasant riches.

If wisdom builds the house, be wary of subtle forms of foolishness which will seek to destroy the house that wisdom built. (Joking at the wrong time may seem innocuous, but can cause offence for example). Prov 14:1 "The wise woman builds her house, but the foolish pulls it down with her hands."

The Fear Of The Lord: The foundation of the house is revealed by the scriptures that state that the beginning of wisdom is the fear of the Lord which encompasses turning away from evil:

Prov 9:10 "The fear of the Lord is the beginning of wisdom".

Ps 111:10 The fear of the Lord is the beginning of wisdom; a good understanding have all those who do His commandments. His praise endures forever.

The enemy of such a sure foundation (the fear of the Lord) is the deception that continuing in sin is entirely permissible for the Christian, which goes against much clear teaching in scripture (Heb 6:4-6; Heb 10:26,27; Col 1:23; Rom 6:1,2,23; 1Cor 6:9,10; Eph 5:5,6; Gal 5:17–19).

People sin when they have little or no fear of the Lord. Holiness and purity (Heb 12:14) are essential for an assured entrance into the Kingdom of Heaven. Therefore permissive sin is a major opponent of godly wisdom. (See later chapters for a discussion on deception.)

Jesus Christ Crucified: The wisdom of God is centred on the cross of Jesus Christ. Jesus Christ is clearly denoted as the cornerstone of the church in the gospels. Christ crucified is the wisdom of God and the demonstration of God's love for us (Rom 5:8). Christ crucified reveals God's love, power and His wisdom in our lives.

1Cor 1:22–24 For Jews request a sign, and Greeks seek after wisdom; but we preach Christ crucified, to the Jews a stumbling block and to the Greeks foolishness, ²⁴ but to those who are called, both Jews and Greeks, Christ the power of God and the wisdom of God.

Therefore we propose that the capstone (or coping stone) of wisdom should be "Jesus Christ Crucified" (Acts 4:11) since this reveals God's wisdom so appropriately to us in the New Testament. This culminated in each believer becoming a temple of the Holy Spirit with the capacity to be led by the Spirit on a regular individual basis. Therefore we need never lack a download of wisdom from God!

One of the benefits of the new covenant is a deeper relationship and dependency upon the Lord. The architecture of wisdom is not to give us a roadmap to become independently "*wise*" so that we reach a place of achievement and pride in our own wisdom. Independent thinking can mistakenly infer that we do not need to pray any more – that is a deception. Godly wisdom is a daily communication with God by His Spirit – Jesus Himself was entirely dependent upon the Father for daily direction and guidance. Jesus stated that "the Son can do nothing of His own accord but only what He sees the Father doing" (John 5:19). And He also said, "*whatever I speak, just as the Father has told Me, so I speak.*" (John 12:50). Our next revelation of wisdom is as close as we are in drawing near to God to worship and fellowship with Him in purity and holiness.

The Seven Pillars: Wisdom has many different facets and aspects to it – to be applied to many varied contexts. The apostle Paul refers to the many facets of wisdom: Eph 3:10 "the manifold (multifaceted) wisdom of God". How do we determine what the other facets of wisdom are? Again we can look to the Bible for our instruction and guidance. Let's look at proverbs chapters 1 and 2 which introduce wisdom to us:

Prov 1:2–4 To know wisdom and instruction, to perceive the words of *understanding*, [3] to receive the instruction of wisdom, *justice, judgment, and equity*; [4] to give prudence to the simple, to the young man *knowledge and discretion* …

Prov 2:2,3,6 So that you incline your ear to wisdom, and apply your heart to understanding; [3] yes, if you cry out for *discernment*, and lift up your voice for understanding, … [6] For the Lord gives wisdom; from His mouth come knowledge and understanding …

The above two sections of scripture open up to us the possibility of describing the 7 pillars as outlined in Figure 1 below.

The seven pillars reveal different aspects of wisdom that we can sometimes overlook. It is instructive to be aware of them in more detail. Wise decision making covers the gamut of every sphere of activity in society, from operating as a sovereign, a judge, a parent or a church leader – this architecture applies in every field. The details behind the selection of each pillar can be found in Appendix A.

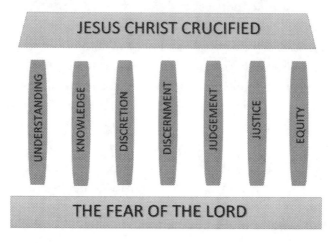

Figure 1: A proposed spiritual architecture outlining the key components of wisdom

CONCLUSION

Even though the scripture emphasizes the importance of wisdom, yet it is not a panacea – we must continually learn to love, obey and rely upon God and asking Him regularly for wisdom each day. Ultimately, *it is more important to learn how to continually rely upon God* than to rely upon our own wisdom and experience. This may sound unusual, but Solomon being the wisest man, strayed and sinned against the Lord (1King 11). And as discussed earlier, it is possible to corrupt sound wisdom.

Wisdom is a tool that assists us in achieving the vision for our lives, and leads us into success with God. With a compelling vision and clear direction filling our heart we embark on the pursuit for greater wisdom and effectiveness as we obey the Lord, seek to be led by His Spirit, and achieve His purposes for our lives.

Prov 12:8 A man will be commended according to his wisdom, but he who is of a perverse heart will be despised.

Chapter Review

The architecture (or description) of the structure of wisdom:

Wisdom with a foundation: The fear of the Lord!

The capstone of wisdom (or the cornerstone): Jesus Christ crucified!

The different components of wisdom: 7 pillars forming a house:

Understanding, Knowledge, Discretion, Ethics, Discernment, Justice, and Judgement.

How Do We Respond?

Think of situations we are in right now - how could extra wisdom help us?

How can we grow in wisdom?

Discuss how can utilising the 7 components of wisdom assist us in our decision making?

How do the Fear of the Lord and "Christ Crucified" assist in providing wise counsel to others?

What happens if we make a habit of not asking others for their wisdom before making certain (unilateral) decisions?

Eccl 8: 5b, 6a ... a wise man's heart discerns both time and judgment, [6] *because for every matter there is a time and judgment ...*

THE PURSUIT OF WISDOM

A daily dependency upon the Lord

Eccl 9: 16, 18 Then I said: "Wisdom is better than strength. Nevertheless the poor man's wisdom is despised, and his words are not heard. ... [18] Wisdom is better than weapons of war; but one sinner destroys much good."

It was November 1993 and I was fast approaching my time limit when I would ask Helen to marry me before she flew back to Malaysia at the end of December, ostensibly never to return to Australia. Helen was still attending a separate church to the Hope Church I was committed to in Melbourne, and she invited me to attend a special meeting one Friday night. Since I was free, I agreed to go, but with some skepticism as I did not respect her church's doctrine, and my pride was evident. I said something tantamount to "What can your church teach me?" Nevertheless, she was patient with me and we entered the hall to listen to the guest speaker called Brother Michael. What ensued was one of the most embarrassing events of my entire life.

The context was that I had a PhD in Physics from Melbourne University and I had been working as Research Fellow for the previous 4 years for

CSIRO (a prestigious government research organization). I was currently one of the leaders in my local church and as a single man I was attempting to impress my girlfriend in order to ask her to marry me. I might have had a "little" pride operating in my life, but I definitely would have denied that, as I had taught on humility at church.

No sooner had we sat down in the second back row of the theatre style seating in this hall and had begun to listen to a few introductory words of the speaker, I began to cry. All attempts to appear respectable and in control were lost. My tears only became more profuse the more I tried to gain composure. This was definitely not a good way to impress Helen. Not only could I not stop crying, it got worse, as my nose started running and I quickly ran out of tissues. Ten minutes went by – still crying next to Helen. Twenty minutes go by – still crying uncontrollably. Finally after more than thirty minutes Brother Michael stopped speaking and I began to regain some dignity. The imposed humiliation succeeded in getting my respect for the speaker, acknowledgement that the Spirit of God was indeed present, and a deeper reality of my own limitations. Helen was overjoyed that I had been humbled in her church meeting! Suffice to say that pride is a hindrance to the pursuit of wisdom.

Prov 11: 2 When pride comes, then comes shame; but with the humble is wisdom.

SECTION A: SEEK AFTER WISDOM

Jesus talks about those virgins who are wise, and those virgins who are foolish:

Matt 25:1 – 5 "Then the kingdom of heaven shall be likened to ten virgins who took their lamps and went out to meet the bridegroom. ² Now five of them were wise, and five were foolish. ³ Those who were foolish took their lamps and took no oil with them, ⁴ but the wise took oil in their vessels with their lamps. ⁵ But while the bridegroom was delayed, they all slumbered and slept."

Note that the differential between wisdom and foolishness in this case is not that some fell asleep – as they all fell asleep. (Definitely in some cases it is unwise to fall asleep – especially at midnight while talking to your wife about something "*urgent*".) In this case it was a simple matter of bringing spare oil, but the spare oil is probably not the real issue either – I suspect it is that the wise were thinking ahead and planning for contingencies, they were "ready". Whereas the foolish were simply going forward to a task or a meeting without forethought indicating a lack of care and diligence, they were "not ready".

How do we grow in wisdom? Moses gives us a succinct summary of our source of wisdom – it is to "be careful to observe" (to do, to obey) the statutes and judgements that the Lord has given us:

Deut 4:5, 6 "Surely I have taught you statutes and judgments, just as the Lord my God commanded me, that you should act according to them in the land which you go to possess. ⁶ Therefore be careful to observe them; for this is your wisdom and your understanding in the sight of the peoples who will hear all these statutes, and say, 'Surely this great nation is a wise and understanding people.'

People should be able to look into a church meeting and make a similar comment today, "Surely these people are wise and understanding in their love for one another!" What do people see when they look inside our church meetings?

Learning from the wisdom of Jesus Christ

Luke 2: 52 And Jesus increased in wisdom and stature, and in favor with God and men.

Donald Trump made the claim in early 2020 regarding Covid-19: "It's going to disappear. One day, it's like a miracle—it will disappear." On June 17ᵗʰ 2020 Trump also made the claim: The pandemic is "fading away. It's going to fade away."[16]. Unfortunately some of our foolish comments are recorded for posterity. Therefore the increasing need for wisdom in our speech and manner is self-evident.

Of course the wonderful example of wisdom is the Lord Jesus Christ Himself, who thwarted so many cunning and devious attacks designed to trick and embarrass Him (Matt 22:15). When confronted in the temple by the chief priests and the elders of the people regarding the source of His authority, He refuted their question with another question (Matt 21:23–27). When he was confronted and questioned by the Pharisees' disciples and the Herodians in front of all the people in the temple regarding the payment of taxes to Rome, He gave the amazing response, *"Render therefore to Caesar the things that are Caesar's, and to God the things that are God's"* (Matt 22:15–22). After this incredible reproof, the Sadducees tried to trick Him about marriage in heaven, but also failed (Matt 22:23–33). Then the Pharisees themselves attacked regarding the greatest commandment (Matt 22:34–40) which Jesus easily answered. Then we see the wisdom of Jesus culminating with His own challenge to the Pharisees asking them who was the Christ (Matt 22:41–46) with the result that no one dared question Him anymore.

The Lord shows us how to operate at a level of wisdom that our opponents will be ashamed. It is possible to achieve higher levels of wisdom if only we treasure it and seek after it. We can pray that the Lord will give us wisdom to gently refute those who seek to deride the Kingdom of God in some derogatory manner.

Demonstrating Wisdom in the Science Arena

When I worked for the Australian Defense Science and Technology Organisation (DSTO) as a Research Scientist (1998 – 2012) I knew I had to present some evidence for the beauty of the design of biological life before my fellow scientists and engineers in their own workplace sooner or

---

[16] Donald Trump, quoted at https://www.theatlantic.com/politics/archive/2020/11/trumps-lies-about-coronavirus/608647/

later. I had already presented some talks on the resurrection of Jesus Christ and reasons on why we believe in God (mainly Easter and Christmas work outreach events). To confront this design question more directly I organized a lunchtime seminar with some of my colleagues with whom we had been running regular bible studies. I emailed the entire 1500 research and engineering staff on the Edinburgh site using the old adage, "Design or Random Chance? Come and join in the discussion!"

While driving to work the morning of the seminar, I felt a word in my heart, "This is why you are here". I knew today would be important as we had 26 scientists and engineers present (one of them a senior principal research leader and a prominent staff member). Most likely they were waiting for an opportunity to pounce on any simplistic scientific arguments presented. My colleagues opened the meeting; another shared a short testimony, and then handed the platform to me.

Waiting to get up to speak, my knees where knocking – yes, like King Belshazzar (Dan 5:6). This had never happened in my life, before or since, that my knees were uncontrollably vibrating. I wondered silently if I might even be able to stand up. The apprehension was incredible. But the time came and I was able to stand and the rapid knee vibrations stopped.

I was also able to fluently present Michael Behe's case for the irreducible complexity of eyesight by going through the biochemical steps of cellular photon detection, to the emission of a negative charge to the optic nerve, to resetting the entire *11-cis-retinal* system ready for the next photon detection[17]. This was the keynote argument against the common position that eyesight had randomly emerged. At the end of my rehearsed presentation, I asked for questions. Not a single question. I was stunned. I asked for comments. Not a single comment. They all just walked away. Wow. That was not what I had expected! Having run this type of seminar in other venues (universities and churches) I was ready for all sorts of emotional diatribes. This was one example in my life when God gave us wisdom that could not be refuted.

---

[17] Michael J. Behe, *"Darwin's Black Box: The Biochemical Challenge to Evolution"*, (1996) Free Press.

The pursuit of money and the cost of wisdom

I was offered a job at Geelong Wool Combing in 1994 with a salary that would be about twice the salary of a position that was offered to me as a research fellow at the Physics Department at Monash University. I chose the job at Monash for a number of reasons – I was not interested in the money (1Tim 6:8, 10, 17).

Job discussed man's love for money in his discourse in chapter 28. It is amazing to see the extent that man will go to in order to seek after money. Some of us study for over 10 years to get a prestigious job so that we can earn more income, but neglect to think much about what constitutes a successful life and marriage. We remain consumed with the pursuit of more dollars and have little time for other priorities. This is not wise.

Job 28:3, 4, 9 – 11 "Man puts an end to darkness, and searches every recess for ore in the darkness and the shadow of death. [4] He breaks open a shaft away from people; in places forgotten by feet … [9] He puts his hand on the flint; he overturns the mountains at the roots. [10] He cuts out channels in the rocks, and his eye sees every precious thing. [11] He dams up the streams from trickling; what is hidden he brings forth to light."

This "miner" in the above verses is a determined person to find more riches that is for sure! But what real value do we place upon God's wisdom? Jesus says He is the "Pearl of Great Price" but what price have we paid to know the Lord in a greater way? Andy Leake sold his house and bought another one so that the church could use the second house for meetings, as it was across the street from our church building. That's a sacrifice. Another man was offered to be given for free a $1.6M holiday house, but he turned it down because he could not leave his church to live in a holiday resort town. What do we do for a higher salary? Have we thought about what sacrifice the Lord might ask of us one day?

Job goes on in his discourse on wisdom almost with a lament when he says:

Job 28: 12, 13 "But where can wisdom be found? And where is the place of understanding? [13] Man does not know its value, nor is it found in the land of the living."

Here we see that the "miner" or the man consumed with financial gain does not appreciate the value of wisdom. Such thinking would be ethereal or irrelevant to such a person. What price would you pay for something you do not value?

What price are we really prepared to pay for wisdom?

Daniel Pink[18] describes the psychological scientific basis for his summary statement that monetary rewards decrease performance, perseverance and intrinsic motivation for a particular activity that requires some level of creativity. This conclusion that giving staff money for making a presentation deadline or completing a special design project (for example) is actually detrimental to their long term intrinsic motivation for their work was revelatory. But companies still persist with such reward based cultures despite the scientific evidence[19]. We find that money cannot buy wisdom nor long term motivation!

Psalm 119:72 "The law of Your mouth is better to me than thousands of coins of gold and silver."

If someone is offered $10M to carry out a certain task there would not be many limitations on the task they would be willing to do. Some would ardently carry out almost any (even illegal) task for $10M. Would we forsake a higher paying job in another city so as to continue to serve in the local church? When have we walked away from our "dream marriage partner" because the Lord was directing us to? When we have given up the job of a lifetime so we can serve God? What price have we paid waiting for the word of the Lord to direct us? Is that wisdom? Yes!

---

[18] Daniel H. Pink, *"Drive: The Surprising Truth about What Motivates us"*, (2009) Riverhead Hardcover.

[19] Daniel H. Pink, *ibid.*

Ps 119:127 Therefore I love Your commandments more than gold, yes, than fine gold!

How often do church leaders leave a church to go to another city because the Lord "suddenly directed them"? Such impulsiveness may not be the best example for our people who are looking for stability in their leaders, which is why wisdom is so important. For church leaders there is a higher price to pay. Can we maintain integrity before God when we change churches because of higher pay? Or if we are an executive leader and our senior pastor is irritating do we suddenly "feel called" elsewhere?

God wants us to be continually led by His Spirit (Rom 8:14; Gal 5:18, 25) not by our emotions or circumstances, but to be obedient and continually dependent upon Him for guidance regarding the next decision (James 1:5). This is the essence of wisdom under the New Covenant.

SECTION B: GROWING IN WISDOM

Chapter 3 outlined the architecture of wisdom which provides a good overall guide for us to grow in wisdom if we are practising each of its components. The foundation of this architecture is the Fear of The Lord:

Psalm 111:10 The fear of the LORD is the beginning of wisdom; a good understanding have all those who do His commandments; and to depart from evil is understanding.

The fear of the Lord is to obey His voice – which is to be led by the Spirit. It is not necessarily showing a one off display of:

the wisdom of Solomon before 2 prostitutes fighting for a baby (1Kin 3), or

the latest strategy from heaven as King David went out to destroy the Philistines (2Sam 5), or

the oracle of God like Ahithophel (2Sam 16:23).

The wisdom we seek after is in the daily decision making that either builds or corrodes relationships, that strengthens or weakens our character, that draws us closer to God or further away.

In Prov 2 we see a few conditions for growth in wisdom (practising the "seven pillars of wisdom"):

Prov 2:1–4 My son, if you receive my words, and treasure my commands within you, ² so that you incline your ear to wisdom, and apply your heart to understanding; ³ yes, if you cry out for discernment, and lift up your voice for understanding, ⁴ if you seek her as silver, and search for her as for hidden treasures;

These conditions are actually quite demanding, as the implication is that these are ongoing requirements, to continue to "*receive, treasure, incline, apply, cry-out, lift-up, seek and search*" which impose upon the student of wisdom a regular heart attitude of each of these actions. Therefore in order to grow in wisdom it requires a long term determination to persevere in seeking, searching, applying, crying, treasuring and receiving words, ideas and thoughts that lead to a greater measure of wisdom. This of course is designed to lead the wise student into the presence of God on a regular basis, asking Him to clarify, explain and elucidate principles, behaviours and hidden motives regarding all sorts of human interactions.

Ask God, "Why did that person say that?", and "What is motivating that person to do such things?" The more we ask, the more we receive. The more we seek, the more we find, and the Lord will show us hidden motives of others if we first prove faithful in dealing with our own hidden motives. Wisdom is a two-edged sword.

Let us determine to grow in faithfulness, diligence, regular dependence upon God in prayer and an insatiable desire to feed on the Word of God:

2Tim 3:15 and that from childhood you have known the Holy Scriptures, which are able to make you wise for salvation through faith which is in Christ Jesus.

It is good to read the entire bible each year for example (I have been doing this almost since my conversion). Some pastors in India read the bible more than once per year. May God birth a heart of love and wisdom to lead His people where the wisdom of God is predicated upon the love of God. Christ Crucified is all about Jesus' love for His people. Proverbs 2 goes on to delineate some of the benefits of searching and seeking for wisdom:

Prov 2:5 – 12 Then you will understand the fear of the Lord, and find the knowledge of God. [6] For the Lord gives wisdom; from His mouth come knowledge and understanding; [7] He stores up sound wisdom for the *upright*; He is a shield to those who *walk uprightly*; [8] He guards the paths of justice, and preserves the way of His saints. [9] Then you will *understand* righteousness and justice, equity and every good path. [10] When *wisdom enters your heart*, and *knowledge is pleasant to your soul*, [11] *discretion* will preserve you; *understanding* will keep you, [12] to deliver you from the way of evil, from the man who speaks perverse things …

This process of growing in wisdom may take place over perhaps a ten year period (varying in dependence upon the individual). Foolishness takes a long time to drive out of us. Ask ourselves how much have we matured and grown wiser over the last ten years?

The scripture above promises that as we make the search and discovery of wisdom a lifelong habit, we will become satisfied with understanding and knowledge. God will shield, guard and preserve our way, and we will be blessed with discretion to escape temptation and discernment to avoid certain people.

The Wise Learn from Their own Mistakes and that of Others!

Learning from other people's mistakes is essential in our pursuit of wisdom, hence reading biographies and specific historical accounts of stressful situations can enlighten us for future contingencies. Even more importantly is to learn from our own mistakes lest we repeat them and the subsequent loss of respect become difficult to regain.

Roy Riegels played centre in the 1929 Rose Bowl game. The game was almost over and the score was very close. Then on one play, Roy suddenly found himself with the ball in his hands, he was not expecting it as part of that stage of the game. Centres know what to do with the ball when they are passing it to the quarterback, but in this case Roy was suddenly uncertain as to what to do. He started running as fast as he could straight for the goal line. He glanced back over his shoulder and saw that he was being frantically pursued by his own teammates. His instincts told him to keep running. Eventually he was tackled by one of his own teammates just short of the opposition's goal line. He was running for the other team's goal line! The other team went on to score and win the game. He went down into ignominious football history – as Wrong Way Riegels![20].

Riegels said years later, "I was embarrassed when I realized what I had done. I wanted a hole to open in the ground so I could jump in it." He was reminded of his mistake throughout his life. He dealt with his situation by laughing about what happened. Riegels once joked "If I had to do it again, I'd still run in the same direction, for I surely thought I was going the right way." He even commented that the whole experience, though mostly embarrassing, disappointing and irritating (people never let him forget) was actually beneficial for him.

Riegels sent letters to athletes who made similar mistakes. He sent a letter to Paramount High School's Jan Bandringa in 1957, who had intercepted a pass only to run it 55 yards into his own end zone. Later Riegels said his blunder made him a better person. "I gained true understanding of life from my Rose Bowl mistake", he said in an interview. "I learned you can bounce back from misfortune and view it as just something adverse that happened to you"[21].

We can learn from our mistakes as Riegels did, or learn from others' mistakes. Let us not be afraid of making mistakes, because that is where progress often hides. But we should be concerned about making the same

---

[20] Roy Riegels, "*Running Hard the Wrong Way*", https://en.wikipedia.org/wiki/Roy_Riegels

[21] Roy Riegels, *ibid.*

mistake regularly. A good discussion on wisdom from a secular viewpoint (without scripture references) is given by *Psychology Today* with some wise practical advice[22].

Intelligence or position do not presuppose wisdom

I knew a man who was trained as a PhD scientist with a senior research position in a prestigious government research organisation – yet his research ideas were narrow minded and a waste of staff man-hours. Another senior research scientist had little imagination and ordered me to conduct experiments which were also a waste of time and produced nothing useful. We can be wise (or foolish) whether we are intelligent or not.

Poor Decisions Can Affect the Remainder of Your Life

An attractive girl came forward after the preaching one Sunday morning some years ago and asked for prayer for guidance. She was thinking of moving interstate to find work. Without praying I said directly to her, "Sometimes moving interstate can be a big mistake if it is not what God wants for us – whether we have a job offer or not. We really need to know God's will in these decisions." She didn't seem to like what I said. I asked her, "Are you willing to stay if God wants you to stay?" Not much response beyond disinterest. So I prayed a general prayer of guidance that the Lord would help her. I kept in touch but her interstate trip did not go well. After about 12 months, instead of getting a job she was a single unemployed mother. Still young – but with a marred future. What is the price of wisdom?

A wise man walks with the wise

Prov 13:20 He who walks with wise men will be wise, but the companion of fools will be destroyed.

---

[22] *Wisdom* Written and Reviewed By Psychology Today Staff https://www.psychologytoday.com/au/basics/wisdom (2009) accessed 8/4/22.

The scripture exhorts us to choose good company, wise mentors and to avoid being unequally joined together (yoked or bound in a covenantal context) to the foolish (1Cor 15:33). I used to drive across the city of Adelaide in order to have a coffee with Ps Norm Reid, an executive pastor in the CRC church in Seaton. I wanted to learn how to be a church leader, to pastor the church, and to understand church planting better. So I needed some face-to-face communication. Ps Norm was gracious to meet with me during the early stages of our church plant. We need to walk with wise men in order to increase in wisdom!

Wise people sharpen each other

Prov 15:22 Without counsel, plans go awry, but in the multitude of counselors they are established.

Prov 27:17 As iron sharpens iron, so a man sharpens the countenance of his friend.

Within our HIM ministry, Ps Wilson and Ps Simon have been particularly strong, ongoing examples of leadership and wisdom. I have also been blessed to meet strong pastors in India and Africa who have helped me grow in spiritual maturity and leadership. Ps Sonny in Liberia, Ps Mapya in DRCongo, Ps Jackson in Bangalore, Ps Ravi in Hyderabad have been particularly inspiring to me over the years. Ps Andrew Evans the apostle of the AOG was a great friend and mentor, and in Perth Ps Benny has been a good source of mentoring. Coffees with Ps Ian Clarkson have been a blessing to help me realign my ethics and values to that of a stalwart Christian leader. We become the sum of so many wise people inputting into our lives.

Bernie Scanlon Was Not A Rich Man

He dedicated himself to fundraising for those less fortunate than him over many years. He even raised money for an orphanage. What a great legacy! Many non-christian families were at his funeral because they knew his genuine love and care for others. Bernie chose to live in a caravan. He only worked to pay his bills, but he travelled all around the world raising money for others! He preached so wisely at his own funeral – he had already laid out discrete program, including the reading out of his own eulogy and sermon! Myself and David Binns (who has been a pastor for many years) were both impressed by the spiritual power of his funeral. The way the two hour service was structured it took people along a journey of his life culminating with a challenge to follow the Lord Jesus Christ. The many non-church goers there were so appreciative of Bernie – there was much love. It was the wisest and most impactful funeral either of us had been to.

The Growth Of Wisdom

There is an ancient Indian legend of a king who loved chess. He challenged visitors to a game, and was usually victorious. One day a traveling sage visited the kingdom and was challenged to a game. To entice him to play, the king offered to give the sage whatever reward he asked if he won. When the king was defeated, to honor his word he asked the sage what prize he would like. The sage asked for one grain of rice to placed on the first square of the chessboard, and then that it be doubled on each following square[23].

The request seemed modest, and the king ordered a bag of rice to be brought. One grain was placed on the first square, two on the second, four on the third, eight on the fourth and so on. But it quickly became apparent the terms of the request were impossible to meet. By the twenty-first square more than one million grains of rice would be required. By the thirty-first square the total would go over one billion—with more than half of the chessboard still left to go.

---

[23] *"The Growth of Wisdom"* by Ministry127, https://ministry127.com/resources/illustration/the-growth-of-wisdom (accessed 8/7/23).

CONCLUSION

Small things have a big impact when they are added together. It is important that we seek God's wisdom for every decision we make, regardless of how small it seems to us. When we incrementally add to our wisdom and understanding, it grows stronger and stronger.

Chapter Review

The pursuit of wisdom is a daily dependency upon the Lord.

Pride hinders the growth of wisdom whereas humility will augment it.

I can apply the architecture of wisdom to my actions and thoughts and see where I need to improve.

The Lord shows us how to operate at a level of wisdom that our opponents are unable to answer.

We find that money cannot buy wisdom nor long term motivation.

The wise learn from their own mistakes and that of others.

Intelligence, age or position do not presuppose wisdom.

Poor decisions can affect the remainder of our lives.

A wise man will seek to walk with the wise. Wise people can sharpen one another.

How Do We Respond?

How would we know that we are not walking in pride? Who would you ask about that?

How many decisions do I make based upon money and salary compared with serving in church?

What mistakes have I made recently that I have learned from?

Do I ascribe wisdom to those in certain positions with a certain educational background?

How can I preclude myself from making poor or even deleterious decisions?

Do I have a mentor or church leader who can correct me and give me advice?

HOW TO GROW IN DISCERNMENT

Some case studies

T he motive to grow in and apply wisdom should be to do God's will, to love Him and others. Going to West Africa not knowing the people you will meet does not sound wise. But if we consider that the wisdom of God is Christ Crucified, then going into the entire world to share the good news and love of God is definitely part of God's wisdom for us.

A Thai pastor reneged twice on his promise to assist with Ps Sonny Brown with his new church plant in Gbarnga, Liberia (West Africa) and left him there hanging with unmet expectations. Leaving me with a 40 minute phone call to placate him from Bangkok in 2006 (not cheap in those days). So I reluctantly decided I would have to go myself, since the family Ps Sonny was connected with were in our church in Adelaide. Feb 2007 was my first trip to Africa, and the first time I had gone further west than Thailand.

My first stop over was in Dubai where I missed the connecting flight, and got stuck in a local airport hotel overnight in a muslim country where I was uncertain if the blades would come out while I was nervously reading my bible in the hotel restaurant. Not knowing the language, not knowing anything about this country, not knowing if the airline bus would even pick me up in the morning – being completely on my own – was all new to me. But don't worry. Things can only get worse.

I eventually caught the flight to Accra, in Ghana, where I successfully missed my connecting flight again because the airport attendant wanted me to walk outside the airport building to catch the next flight – but I was unwilling to leave my luggage into his trust! So I went inside to get the luggage (like a normal westerner), missed the flight, got stuck in Accra, missed 3 nights of crusade meetings in Gbarnga with 400 people waiting for me – much to the chagrin of Ps Sonny. This trip was off to a good start.

Finally I arrived at the airport servicing Liberia's capital city, Monrovia. I probably should check up on my history next time. I didn't realise that Liberia had only just come out of a brutal 12 year civil war with over 1M casualties and atrocities. The city had been burned and looted. The airport was a shell of what it used to be with most of the previous buildings either burned or broken down. Looking outside my plane window as we slowed on the tarmac, I saw a lot of grass, and a small wooden shack that looked like a large garage. I was shocked. "Where am I?" Coming from the massive airport terminal in Dubai only added to my estranged feelings and uncertainty. While going through customs someone tried to grab my bag – I nervously pushed their hand away, not wanting to offend too much as I was really not sure how to handle a confrontation in this place! I nervously walked outside the airport terminal, and came face to face with what looked like about 500 angry African men. I kept walking, acting as if I knew what I was doing; hoping to God that Ps Sonny was not late!

Feeling the intimidation and rejection beginning to tangibly grip my heart, I kept praying. "Where am I? Why am I here? Oh my goodness!" Suddenly a total stranger rushed up to me and said "Quick get into the car!" I was obliging for this rescue, but "Sorry, who are you?" "I'm Ps Sonny" came the terse reply, while he gave strong directions to the driver to leave the airport immediately. Out of the pan, into the fire. The more we drove, the more we spoke, the more I was able to relax. Whew. Sonny was a man of God and it was good to be here. I tried to take photos of the machine guns menacingly sticking out of the UN Guard posts as we drove past. It was about a 4 hour drive weaving between pot holes with continuous breaking and accelerating, the jerking being broken up by the bumps we regularly encountered on the cratered road.

The first night we had a short meeting inside a small church building made from bamboo sticks and branches. I drank some lemonade after the meeting, and noticed a little water on the top of the can. That night I descended into an agony of vomiting and dry retching, getting up five times during the night and thrusting my face into a filthy toilet bowl. My low tolerance for pain got the better of me and like Jonah I prayed to die. I was so weak. The next morning Ps Sonny needed me to go back into the capital city and exchange the travellers cheques I had brought for cash. So began a 4 hour agony in the heat of the day, feeling too weak to eat anything, afraid to drink the water – not knowing what caused my vomiting. Then we waited inside a bank for about 3 hours while they decided what to do with the "white man's" travellers cheques. The whole city seemed dishevelled, unkempt, uninviting and unfriendly. I did not want to be there. Then after acquiring the precious dollars, we set out again. This time my energy level continued to plummet in the heat and the thought of eating was revolting to me. Surely death would be better than this 11 hour agony. "When can I die?" I bemoaned.

While driving back to Gbarnga I wondered who would preach at the evening meeting, as by now I would be too late. Then I wondered who would pray for the sick. I was plotting how to entirely avoid the meeting in my mind. Finally we arrived. I sheepishly walked into the back of the small building lit by a few small globes strung from the ceiling powered by a petrol generator chugging loudly outside and the white teeth of smiling greetings from the church members. "Welcome to Ps Brendan! He is going to pray for the sick for us!" I couldn't believe what I heard. I could barely stand up myself. I tried to pray for someone, but my voice was barely audible – I could hardly speak. I tried to shout, but it only came out as a whisper, "Be healed in Jesus' name!" I felt so weak. But I was being obedient. After praying for a few people I sat down in exhaustion. Then I felt this overwhelming urge to vomit right there in the meeting, in front of everyone. "Oh no!" I cried in my heart. "God I cannot vomit here, it will be a total failure and disgrace! God you have to help me! Oh Lord, You have to heal me please!" As soon as I prayed I stood up and I was healed. Nobody noticed except me! No more fever, no more assailing weakness, my headache was clear. I had some strength, and no vomiting. Thank God! Welcome to West Africa for the sake of the Gospel!

Wisdom is not always obvious, but is vindicated by her children. We have over 26 HIM churches with 1500 people in West Africa today.

Remember that discernment comes from the Spirit of God:

1Cor 2:13, 14 These things we also speak, not in words which man's wisdom teaches but which the Holy Spirit teaches, comparing spiritual things with spiritual. The natural man does not receive the things of the Spirit of God, for they are foolishness to him; nor can he know them, because they are spiritually discerned.

SECTION A: WISDOM ANTICIPATES AND DISCERNS HOW PEOPLE WILL BEHAVE

First Scenario: You are not happy with your boss. His management of your work has been poor, and he relates to you in a distant and condescending manner; he seems insecure about his own lack of knowledge in the field you're working in. Having prayed and you feel it is OK with the Lord; you approach your boss and ask for a transfer to another group. You expect your boss might be disappointed to lose you – but he seems immediately happy, he smiles and wishes you all the best, all too eagerly – as if he is glad you are leaving. Wisdom perceives that this boss is hiding his sense of loss and is attacking back with a charming smile to hurt you (to make you feel that he doesn't need you), as if he is happy you are going. This can be a mechanism insecure people use to protect themselves, to counter-attack so as to give the appearance of strength – but this is small minded and poor leadership.

Second Scenario: A colleague walks past you in the cafeteria without acknowledging that they have seen you. Upon reflection, you realise that before you looked up in their direction they had sufficient time to notice you then to look away. The pretense of "not seeing you" makes you suspicious that this person cannot be trusted. As a result in future conversations with this colleague you are more cautious about disclosing any personal weaknesses or vulnerabilities.

Wisdom Looks at a Situation and Studies People

Once we accurately discern a person's attitude (and its components), then we can begin to predict how the person will respond under pressure, success, failure, exposure, prominence and other situations. So we postulate in our mind a psychological equation:

This person has Attitude X and therefore we predict to see evidence of Behaviour Y. Actual observation is Behaviour Z

Of course our prediction will be inaccurate at times or even wrong. We were expecting behavior of type Y but observed Z. So rather than give up on our journey of increasing accuracy in discernment, we work backwards from Z. Let's say Z consisted of the observation of timidity and insecurity, but we had discerned that the prevailing Attitude X was anger. Perhaps either our discernment of X was incorrect and we need to practice correlating our discernment with expected behavior. Or perhaps there was more at play in Attitude X than just anger. Maybe we can postulate a fear of rejection to be operating as well – in which case we need to refine our discernment and pattern match over time more often so that we can predict the resulting behavior more consistently.

For example:

We discern an angry attitude (countenance) and predict an unforgiving response to people's mistakes. We watch and see over time how accurate our initial discernment was by specific reactions to mistakes. Then we reassess and refine our discernment by pattern matching in our mind.

We discern a non-transparent smile (they seem to be hiding something) so we predict to observe deceitful behavior. The hypocrite can be revealed by contradictions between spoken assurances and resultant actions.

We suspect an insincere motive upon receiving multiple gifts, so we predict manipulation, control or demands for unearned intimacy. This is similar to flattery, so the unsuspecting person becomes manipulated and deceived unless aware of this process (see later chapters on deception).

So in the above re-modelling of our equation, the expectations are iterated and then we learn to be more observant, picking up cues that previously hid the pain of rejection. In this way we are learning to trigger our discernment in a wiser fashion. Learning to discern controlling, manipulating, charming and dominating tendencies is fundamental. If we look at some more basic examples:

We discern *Attitude X:*		We predict *Behaviour Y:*
If a person seems proud,	expected response might be	"I told you so. I am right!"
If a person seems selfish,	"	"I don't care"
If a person seems hurt,	"	"It is your fault!"
If a person seems guilty,	"	"I don't know"
If a person seems blamed	"	"Go on, it's all my fault"
If a person seems to lack attention	"	"You don't love me!"
If a person seems unappreciated	"	"You never compliment me!"
If a person seems deceitful	"	"I have done nothing wrong".
If a person seems wise	"	"let's work together through this"

Wisdom will seek to bring about restoration, unity, good will and harmony. Wisdom does not resort to intimidation or anger which are often responses from a selfish perspective. Wisdom will often ask the question: *"What do I want to achieve here?"*

When we are wise, we will choose the best option for a response from God's perspective: which is to show love, grace, acceptance, kindness, understanding, consideration for other's weaknesses, to pursue peace, and to honour God in all things.

Responses Under Pressure

Our response needs to consider, *"What do I want to achieve in this situation?"* We can be harsh and complain, "You are late!", or we might respond and say "It is good to see you."

If we are unwisely harsh in a *social* setting, it can create an atmosphere where people behave out of fear (when we are actually intending to build a culture of acceptance) and they don't want to participate. But setting a standard in a *leadership* meeting is building a culture of respect and accountability, which is essential of course. Therefore our response under pressure considers the setting, and what we desire to achieve.

In a team context, the culture of the organization or church needs to be clearly outlined by a set of values. For example, the leadership can train their people, so that instead of manipulating people, they develop their people to have an intrinsic motivation. Likewise, rather than to dominate them, seek to empower and delegate; instead of practicing charm, determine to be a person of integrity; rather than indulge an insecure urge to control, provide the spiritual covering of a loving parental authority. These values need to be embodied (modelled), taught and protected within any church, company or volunteer organization that seeks to emulate them.

If a team value is to respect other people's time, then being punctual becomes an important part of the culture of the team, and needs to be guarded.

SECTION B: WISDOM HELPS US TO KNOW
WHAT TO SAY AND WHAT NOT TO SAY

God does not want us to tell people all their problems all at once – we get tempted to when we are upset and behaving unwisely.

John 16:12 "I still have many things to say to you, but you cannot bear them now".

Eph 4:15 '…but, speaking the truth in love, may grow up in all things into Him who is the head…'

Wisdom will moderate what we say

Depending upon a person's background, relative knowledge, experiences, misconceptions, problems, weaknesses or level of interest in a particular subject we will adjust our conversation.

Background: Culture, environment and upbringing will develop certain expectations of etiquette which should be acknowledged and observed if a successful liaison is to follow, e.g. cross generational communication or a westerner relating to a Japanese with a sense of decorum and propriety.

Relative Knowledge: If someone knows much more than we do, try not to discuss basic issues with them, lest we offend them. Yet if someone does not know some basic principles in a certain field, then we need to go over those in an understanding way (e.g. a medical doctor to a child).

Experiences: If someone has been through a war and seen numerous deaths, then discussing a minor car accident may not endear them to us. Determine their experiences and relate on their level, discuss what captures their imagination, not our own.

Misconceptions: Try to determine as soon as possible if a person has strong points of view that disagree with our own (e.g. "All paths lead to God" or "We cannot eat meat"). It may be wise to come back to an issue later after having built a basic level of friendship, rather than confronting sensitive issues prematurely.

Problems: If a person has experienced familial abuse, rape or divorce, then these topics need to either be avoided, or if the person raises them, to be discussed in a very sensitive, compassionate, understanding manner (e.g. a careless comment regarding one of these areas could cause insult and shame).

Weaknesses: Be circumspect with respect to people's weaknesses, and try our best not to make a harsh judgement (Rom 15:1). With those who are doubting, anxious, or insecure, we need to be especially careful in our treatment of comments directed in these areas. To someone who is angry (and has not practised managing their emotions), a comment like "Just keep calm!" can be too confrontational and demanding for them, and can escalate a conflict.

Level of Interest: Try not to discuss your favourite topic with those who are not interested! This is easily done if we are over enthusiastic and assume people have the same likes or dislikes as ourselves. We should not assume people are interested in our hobbies or our problems. (I get phone calls from people and before I can say "How are you?" they launch into a discourse describing their latest list of personal traumas – this is unwise.) Discuss with people their concerns, experiences and passions – listen carefully and seek to genuinely understand them. Then later, bring along our own vision and dreams for discussion.

Avoidable Conflict

Sometimes we may feel an urge to speak a directive comment to a person we know which is unnecessary. We should be slow to address other's problems or weaknesses – most people are starving for appreciation and kindness. *Wisdom takes the encouraging approach unless otherwise directed.* If specifically asked, we may make a comment regarding a character trait. If presumptuous words are spoken without love, people can be offended very easily because of the sensitivity of the area concerned. This can result in precious, long term relationships being damaged by resentment or even severed by bitterness.

The Apostle Paul's Strategy for Building Bridges

Paul the wise master builder grew into becoming *"all things to all men"*. He outlined for us his wise strategy of relating to many different people groups (1Cor 9:19 – 23). Beginning with his own position as *"free from all men"* he delineates a series of attitudes in order to relate to varying people groups:

- "I have made myself a servant to all, that I might win the more" (take a humble attitude and be a servant);

1Cor 10:23 … but not all things edify.

- "To the Jews I became as a Jew, that I might win Jews" (adopt their culture – I recently ate dinner with my fingers while visiting an Indian family in Fiji);
- "To those who are under the law, as under the law, that I might win those who under the law" (follow their rules – observe a Sabbath day or some unusual dietary regulations);

1Cor 6:12 All things are lawful for me, but all things are not helpful. All things are lawful for me, but I will not be brought under the power of any.

- "To those who are without law, as without law (not being without law toward God, but under law toward Christ), that I might win those who are without law" (be respectful towards people and validate their opinions and viewpoints);
- "To the weak I became as weak, that I might win the weak" (honour all men – by not condemning, being judgmental or critical of them);

1Cor 8:9, 13 But beware lest somehow this liberty of yours become a stumbling block to those who are weak. Therefore, if food makes my brother stumble, I will never again eat meat, lest I make my brother stumble.

- "I have become all things to all men that I might by all means save some" (maintain integrity before man and God, but seek to comprehend and empathise with all).

Rom 14:20, 21 Do not destroy the work of God for the sake of food. ... [21]It is good neither to eat meat nor drink wine nor do anything by which your brother stumbles or is offended or is made weak.

- "Now this I do for the gospel's sake, that I may be partaker of it with you." The motive for everything we do is for God and His kingdom, including our motive to be wise and successful.

CONCLUSION

There are many subcategories of when wisdom is important for the maturing Christian to take notice. During the 2007 combined military exercise called Talisman Sabre, I was assigned as a Scientific Observer for Combined Command and Control structures for a week on the Helicopter Landing Dock (LHD) the USS Essex. It is a US warship with a staff of about 3,000 military personnel. This LHD had the tag line "*Take Notice!*" This is like a "Warning!" sign. The scriptures give us many examples and warnings where wisdom is imperative in order to avoid the consequences of foolishness.

Chapter Review

Those who are wise:

Practise discerning people's attitudes, anticipate how they will act or react, observe their behaviour and then refine their initial discernment.

Practise choosing what to say, when and how; and what not to say.

Practice slowing down their reactions and responses and plan what to say and do under pressure!

Wisdom will moderate what we say depending upon a person's: background, relative knowledge, experiences, misconceptions, problems, weaknesses or level of interest in a particular subject.

We need to practise these principles in order to become more wise.

Wisdom is very precious. When we contrast it with foolishness (and its cost in damages) we begin to realise how precious wisdom is.

How Do We Respond?

Application of Wisdom: How do I practically apply wisdom?

The most important facet of our lives is our faith in God. How am I growing in my faith?

Have I given my heart fully to the Lord Jesus Christ?

The beginning of wisdom is to fear God, and to have faith in the Lord Jesus Christ – because Jesus Christ crucified is the power of God and the wisdom of God.

God can give us wisdom to become wise master-builders, amen!

1Cor 3:9, 10 For we are God's fellow workers; you are God's field, you are God's building. [10] According to the grace of God which was given to me, as a wise master builder I have laid the foundation, and another builds on it.

APPLYING WISDOM
Choosing a Spouse and Building a Strong Marriage!

T he prophet John Jacks called Helen and myself out the front of all the people at our Hope Church camp during Easter 1997. He began eloquently giving a word to encourage us from the Lord. He said "God has put you two together!" This was a good confirmation for me, as John had spoken the word *"You need a wife!"* over me in front of the entire Hope Melbourne church leadership in November of 1992, 3 months before I met Helen (on the 19th Feb 1993) – at which the whole congregation had burst out laughing! On this latter occasion, he went on to encourage me that God had a ministry for me beyond that local church. He then leaned forward as if for emphasis, and said, "You need to listen to your wife – *she has wisdom that surpasses logic!*" Again the church cracked up laughing! Of course Helen has levered this to her advantage ever since!

There is a wisdom that surpasses logic, that is essential for church leadership, but there is also an area of wisdom for the husband in relating to his wife. Often husbands (especially me) will come up with "good ideas" that sound great, but are actually not that wise. For example while we were on holidays in Fiji and meant to be spending time together, I sneaked out of the hotel room early on a Sunday morning and went to preach at a local

C3 church in Nadi! I thought that was a "great idea" but didn't dare tell Helen until days later!

A good marriage requires the husband and wife to increase in wisdom as to how to grow and build a strong relationship. After 10 years of training in physics at Melbourne University and another 4 and a half years of stressful research at CSIRO I had no idea how ill-equipped I was to enter into a marriage. All of my life had been taken up with study and work (with tennis thrown in when I was free) and in later years, my walk with the Lord. I had no idea how to build a strong relationship with the woman who had become my wife! Once the honeymoon was over, the harsh reality of my insensitivity to Helen set in. I needed wisdom to relate to her, and "I needed it now!"

Many relational conflicts ensued while I was juggling my values between serving and honoring God and honoring my wife. My understanding of the two and how they fit together took years to learn, especially when we became the leaders of our church plant in Adelaide – learning how to lead my wife as a pastor and a husband yet to respect her as a church leader in her own right was problematic, stressful and a real cause that led me to seek wisdom. I knew God wanted us to have a beautiful loving marriage, because that is His generic plan and purpose for every marriage – but how to achieve that in the battlefield of church planting while we were both working 5 days a week was a challenge.

Ps Simon Eng (HIM Elder and former president) gave me a strong wakeup call while giving us both some brief counselling around 2002, saying, "Without your wife you do not have a ministry!" I never forgot that, and tried to learn more wisdom. Many a time I would silently ask, "Please God help me now!" while in the midst of yet another misunderstanding caused by my own selfishness and insensitivity to Helen's needs. God showed me the cross (Gal 2:20). "Hmm. Is there a better way to build a loving relationship?" I wrestled. Eph 5:27 "Husbands love your wives"!

Wisdom Can Be Contrary to What Seems "Reasonable"

M. Niranjan posted an interesting anecdote about two girls sitting for their Standard 12 exams in Maharashtra, India[24]. They decided not to do well in their final exams by deliberately failing them, because they did not want to be sent to the big city to further their studies, then to eventually marry a professional who would be working night and day for the rest of their lives trying to pay off expensive bills. They thought it would be better to stay in the country, marry a farmer, have a peaceful life and avoid the intense stress and expectations of city life.

This decision depended upon how much they valued a peaceful life and whether they loved country life compared with city life, and that value caused them to choose carefully where to live and who to marry.

Who we marry is an important decision and the values of the person we marry need to be scrutinized assiduously otherwise a discord in vision and direction in life can result, which only diminishes the quality of the marriage. So it is not just a matter of "being in love" with someone, but finding a person who is entirely compatible in terms of values and vision, so that there can be agreement in decision making. My wife Helen left her successful job as an accountant at Merrick Webster in Melbourne to go to Adelaide (without a job) to help me start a church with a few people. Her values and vision matched with mine, so the sacrifice was made without any argument or discord at all.

Going back to Niranjan's anecdote above where exam failure was a chosen option, in some cases, it might be wise not to get promoted in a career-ambitious company that expects excessive dedication to the job. Again it comes back to our set of values. If we live for career success then clearly promotion is the goal – and that can be good for a phase in our lives. But if we want to spend more time with our wife and family, volunteer for church activities or leadership meetings, then getting promoted might

---

[24] M. Niranjan; University of Mumbai (1996), "*Two Girls From A Village Are Heading For The Std. XII Exams*". Taken from https://www.quora.com/profile/Niranjan-M-52

steer us away from those values. In some cases career success can be the worst thing for us.

What other relationship exists where we can prove that we love God by loving another person?

1 John 3:16 By this we know love, because He laid down His life for us. And we also ought to lay down our lives for the brethren.

God commands us to lay our lives down for our husband or wife (Eph 5:22 – 32) so marriage plays a crucial part in revealing His love to mankind:

1 John 4:7 – 11 Beloved, let us love one another, for love is of God; and everyone who loves is born of God and knows God. [8] He who does not love does not know God, for God is love. [9] In this the love of God was manifested toward us, that God has sent His only begotten Son into the world, that we might live through Him. [10] In this is love, not that we loved God, but that He loved us and sent His Son to be the propitiation for our sins. [11] Beloved, if God so loved us, we also ought to love one another.

In the light of these verses we see that marital love requires perseverance, forgiveness and sacrifice if it is to prevail over the tests of time and temptation. True love from God can be shed abroad in our heart (Rom 5:5) as we follow His ways and honour the wife of our youth (Mal 2:14 – 16). Romantic love is centred upon having my own dreams and desires fulfilled, and my own expectations being met. Romantic love "makes me feel good", but if we seek "feelings" we will be disappointed. God's love encompasses laying down our lives for others, not being self-willed or self-seeking.

Remember that satan will attempt to destroy your marriage any way he can. Satan plans to deceive and divide, whereas God seeks truth, love and unity. God desires to bless your marriage with love, joy and peace – but we must honour God and follow His ways.

Dating and Marriage Charts!

These four charts are outlined below. They are not meant to be a complete description of all of the factors involved, but provide a (somewhat humorous) outline of some salient points. The titles of the four charts are:

How to easily make an unwise choice of a marriage partner.

How to wisely choose a good marriage partner.

How to have a bad marriage.

How to have a great marriage.

CONCLUSION

Marriage is an important vehicle to reveal God's love and holiness. As a husband and wife love each other faithfully over many years they demonstrate God's love and kindness:

John 13:34, 35 A new commandment I give to you, that you love one another; as I have loved you, that you also love one another. [35] By this all will know that you are My disciples, if you have love for one another."

Chapter Review

In this chapter I hope to impart the importance of marriage – that the "marriage bed is holy" before God and although our society largely holds nothing sacred – yet God holds marriage as sacred. But like all relationships – it takes wisdom, time and patience to build a beautiful marriage. Love is our motivation and servanthood and deferring to one another is the manifestation of that love. It is possible to have our hearts filled with peace and joy each day with our spouse, amen. The four charts below are meant to be useful guideposts as to what to avoid, and what to practice in our courting days and marriage relationships.

How Do We Respond?

Pastor Ian Clarkson made the comment that "if you are the man, make sure your lifestyle is cherishing your wife so she knows she is always first in your heart even if you go to work every day with pretty young secretaries around you showing off their 'wares'. And you nourish her in every way spiritually, sexually, mentally, and socially"[25].

"If you are the lady and wife, make sure your man feels honored by you so that if he might get cut down and humiliated with failure he knows the one who loves him most, knows him best and looks up to him no matter what"[26].

The above comment provides us with a good guide and litmus test as to how supporting we are of our spouse during difficult times.

Eph 5: 33 Nevertheless let each one of you in particular so love his own wife as himself, and let the wife see that she respects her husband.

---

[25] Rev Ian Clarkson, Chairman, Hopenet SA Inc, Founder of Branches Church, Adelaide. Generate Foundational Standing Committee. Chairman of the board of Barnabas Fund Australia. Personal communication.
[26] Rev Ian Clarkson *ibid*.

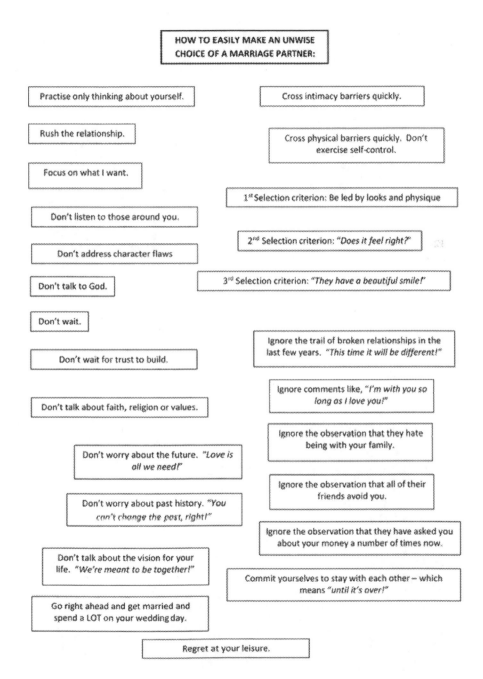

HOW TO EASILY MAKE AN UNWISE CHOICE OF A MARRIAGE PARTNER:

Practise only thinking about yourself.

Cross intimacy barriers quickly.

Rush the relationship.

Cross physical barriers quickly. Don't exercise self-control.

Focus on what I want.

1st Selection criterion: Be led by looks and physique

Don't listen to those around you.

2nd Selection criterion: *"Does it feel right?"*

Don't address character flaws

3rd Selection criterion: *"They have a beautiful smile!"*

Don't talk to God.

Don't wait.

Ignore the trail of broken relationships in the last few years. *"This time it will be different!"*

Don't wait for trust to build.

Ignore comments like, *"I'm with you so long as I love you!"*

Don't talk about faith, religion or values.

Ignore the observation that they hate being with your family.

Don't worry about the future. *"Love is all we need!"*

Ignore the observation that all of their friends avoid you.

Don't worry about past history. *"You can't change the past, right!"*

Ignore the observation that they have asked you about your money a number of times now.

Don't talk about the vision for your life. *"We're meant to be together!"*

Commit yourselves to stay with each other – which means *"until it's over!"*

Go right ahead and get married and spend a LOT on your wedding day.

Regret at your leisure.

HOW TO WISELY CHOOSE A GOOD MARRIAGE PARTNER:

Ask God to direct you

Seek wise counsel – ask parents, mature friends, church leaders

"Am I at a mature marriageable place without dysfunctional bad habits?"

Wait for God's timing for you ~ for some phases in life it is simply inadvisable to get married

Check their character ~ ask direct questions.

Check with God specifically about this person ~ this might take many sessions of prayer

Check my own heart motive ~ my desires first or God's kingdom first?

Be willing to let the relationship go if God directs.

Check their history of relationships and ask *"Why did this one not work out?"*

Build mutual trust slowly through many detailed challenging conversations.

Talk about the future, your expectations, core values, and your shared vision frequently!

Watch their words and comments carefully – ask questions!

Check for previous examples in their life demonstrating commitment.

Watch how they relate to your family and friends – especially when they think no-one is watching.

Watch how they handle subjects such as money, job, career, looks and popularity?

Check for signs of poor ability to commit: changing jobs frequently, half-finished projects, half-finished studies, changes in their mind easily.

Watch how they (react) handle the situation when you are late again.

Check whether divorce is an option in their thinking?

Watch for when they get angry – *"Am I willing to live with this weakness?"*

After it seems that boxes are being ticked – check again – *"Is this really God's will for you?"*

How will I know if it is God's will? What experience do I have in discerning God's will from my own will?

Do others notice an increase in joy and peace in my life?

Plan for your wedding day ~ but do not rush it, and try not to get stressed!

Get married, invite everybody and celebrate God's goodness!

Persevere in love with much patience and forgiveness!

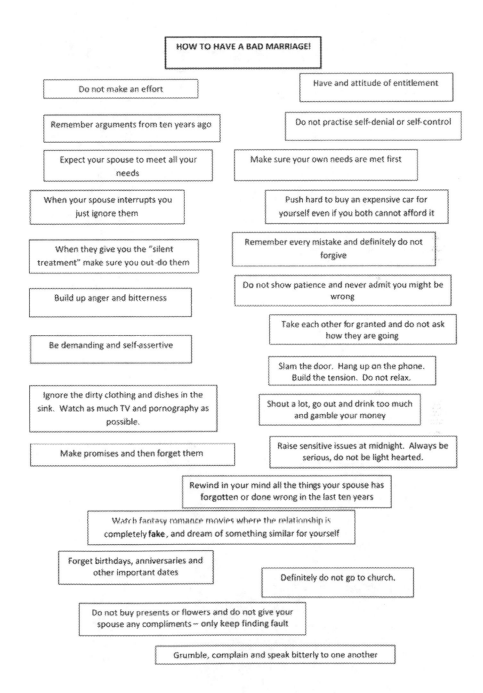

HOW TO HAVE A BAD MARRIAGE!

Do not make an effort

Have and attitude of entitlement

Remember arguments from ten years ago

Do not practise self-denial or self-control

Expect your spouse to meet all your needs

Make sure your own needs are met first

When your spouse interrupts you just ignore them

Push hard to buy an expensive car for yourself even if you both cannot afford it

When they give you the "silent treatment" make sure you out-do them

Remember every mistake and definitely do not forgive

Build up anger and bitterness

Do not show patience and never admit you might be wrong

Take each other for granted and do not ask how they are going

Be demanding and self-assertive

Slam the door. Hang up on the phone. Build the tension. Do not relax.

Ignore the dirty clothing and dishes in the sink. Watch as much TV and pornography as possible.

Shout a lot, go out and drink too much and gamble your money

Make promises and then forget them

Raise sensitive issues at midnight. Always be serious, do not be light hearted.

Rewind in your mind all the things your spouse has forgotten or done wrong in the last ten years

Watch fantasy romance movies where the relationship is completely **fake**, and dream of something similar for yourself

Forget birthdays, anniversaries and other important dates

Definitely do not go to church.

Do not buy presents or flowers and do not give your spouse any compliments – only keep finding fault

Grumble, complain and speak bitterly to one another

HOW TO HAVE A GREAT MARRIAGE!

Spend time with one another

Treasure your moments together because life is busy and short.

Speak kind words to each other every day

Say "*I love you!*" often. Pursue love with one another.

Practise being very slow to get angry

Forgive everything – deliberately erase mistakes from your mind!

Think about all the good things they have done for you

Don't be rude or insensitive, remember what upsets them.

Remember important dates – be generous with presents and flowers

Never allow the "silent treatment" to last very long! Calmly discuss issues.

Do not make promises you know you cannot keep!

Do not get anxious or jealous over "competitors", trust in the loyalty of your spouse

Build trust by fulfilling your word every day

Choose carefully the day/time to address issues or to raise grievances

Build trust by patiently addressing issues at the wisest time

Build trust through vulnerable intimacy: "Honey I was attracted to this other person yesterday!"

Take time off work for your spouse – do not be too busy

Treasure your marriage more than your car, house, clothes or career.

Show love to your spouse in front of your children and others.

Choose your words carefully and wisely when you are upset – never shout or raise your voice in anger.

Pray to God continually and ask Him for wisdom to understand your spouse and to know what to say and when

Pray to God to change you to be less selfish and to be more others-centred.

Definitely go to church regularly. Encourage other couples to love each other too

Be willing to sacrifice your life for your spouse or your children

Spend time in prayer and bible reading asking the Lord to soften your heart to make you more loving and to be a person of integrity and honour

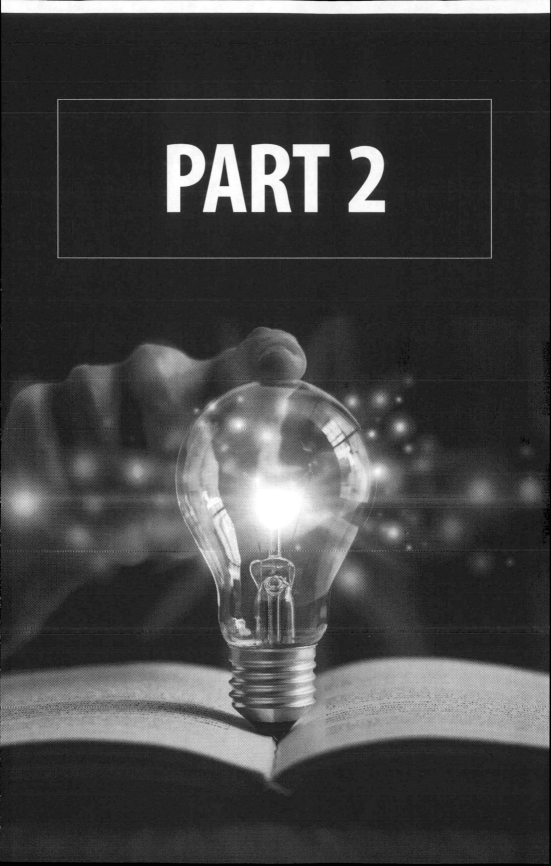

PART 2

WHAT IS DECEPTION?

Consequences and famous cases

---

2 Cor 11:3 But I fear, lest somehow, as the serpent deceived Eve by his craftiness, so your minds may be corrupted from the simplicity that is in Christ.

---

t was February 1992. A few friends and I lingered behind at the wooden table after the lunch with church people at Papa Gino's pizza café in Lygon St, Carlton, Melbourne. It had been a fairly uneventful lunch with the normal conversational buzz of fellowship and fun. But as a particular girl left the pizza café laughing loudly with one of the other guys, one of my friends, Ben Frawley, leaned my way and sarcastically commented, "So you were deceived weren't you!" I was cornered by the reality of life – I had sincerely previously thought that the girl who had just left was "God's will for me". I looked straight back at him and in front of the other two, replied without a doubt "Yes". That represented a pivotal breakthrough phase for me after four and a half years of a certain train of thought, conviction, emotional investment and energy – that I had been wrongly guided in my spiritual discernment. It had been a very difficult few years – to say the least. But I know that the Lord used that time to develop and strengthen me through that fire – meditating on the Word became a life-line, not merely a good spiritual habit. God's word became alive to me, and brought me up by His Spirit to help me continue to persevere by faith.

Being deceived is no small matter. Although I appeared to diminish its import with my brief answer to my friend, yet it had devastated my life for over 4 years. I would not want anyone to go through similar struggles. To admit I was wrong and had been deceived was in reality a relief. The truth will set us free, thank God! (John 8:32).

Just to clarify for my readers: you may ask – "How does someone who teaches on deception become deceived himself?" Briefly, in 1987 I was a young (less than 3 years old) Christian, born again into a church with a doctrinal weakness, with a "dating revelation". This was where single people in the church could not date or even go out with each other; but were expected to seek God's will as Isaac and Rebecca did. This opened some of the single people up to the activity of deceiving romantic spirits. It is also important to grasp – that none of us are immune to deception. By 1990 that whole church movement had disbanded.

SECTION A: *WHAT IS TRUTH?*

Truth is that which is true, or in accordance with fact or reality; "a fact or belief that is accepted as true." *Pilate said to Jesus Christ, "What is truth?" (John 18:38).* A fundamental fact of the nature of our universe is that some things are true, and other things are false. *Truth is reflected by or corresponds to reality.* What is false does not. There can be many false ideas surrounding one true statement.

Isaiah 59:14 Justice is turned back, and righteousness stands afar off; for *truth is fallen in the street*, and equity cannot enter.

Isaiah lamented that truth had "*fallen in the street*". If truth is cast off and treated so badly, then the consequences can be horrendous. What is the abyss? The Abyss in this context represents the variety of consequences of deception – where deception will lead us if we are not wise.

We fondly remember a young man who began attending our church meetings and would fellowship with us afterwards at the Golden Grove Café in north east Adelaide. He used to repeat to us, *"All things are true!"* It was quite humorous to try to talk him out of this, he would simply reply, *"Yes, that's true!"* We met him again about ten years later during some evangelism in the city and he had been soundly converted, thank God!

Types of Truth

Jeremiah laments about the state of his people in Jerusalem late in the 7th century BC when he writes "Do not trust in these lying words … Behold, you trust in lying words that cannot profit. … Truth has perished and has been cut off from their mouth!" (Jer 7:4, 8, 28). Truth will always need to be contended for (Jude 3) as it will be constantly attacked by a phalanx (an impenetrable military attack formation) of lies.

What are different types of truth? (Five types of truth can be discussed: Correspondence, Coherence, Pragmatic, Redundancy and Semantic theories of truth. These are discussed in a UK Essay[27]). For our discussion here we will look at a brief outline of the following:

Scientific truth: reproducible experiments, consistent laws of behaviour.

Historical truth: documentation of a series of events, careful transcription of historical documents, archaeological evidence and artefactual evidence.

Legal truth: based on eyewitness testimonies, circumstantial evidence or corroborating documentation etc. Laws can be changed, but truth is an enduring legal quality that is to be ardently pursued.

Mathematical truth: 2 + 2 = 4 is based on standard (Euclidian) geometric axioms. These axioms are the basic description of a mathematical domain. If we change these axioms then we change the geometry, and truth

---

[27] UKEssays. (November 2018). *The Five Main Theories Of Truth.* Retrieved from https://www.ukessays.com/essays/philosophy/the-five-main-theories-of-truth-philosophy-essay.php?vref=1

statements can vary, and 1 + 1 = 1 for example, becomes possible. Rota writes: "A mathematical system consists of axioms, primitive notions, a notation, and rules of inference. A mathematical statement is held to be true if it is correctly derived from the axioms by applications of the rules of inference"[28]. Consistency in the applications of the rules of "inference" then becomes paramount in the pursuit of mathematical truth. There is no room for emotional application of these rules or axioms. Kant has stated along similar lines that mathematical truth embodies: "The conformity of a thought to the laws of logic; in particular, in a concept, consistency; in an inference, validity; in a proposition, agreement with assumptions."[29].

Absolute Truth: that which is true for all people, for all places, for all time. Gimbel writes: "What exactly is an absolute truth? An absolute truth is a concept or idea that is true no matter what, such as the rule that a circle can never be square"[30].

A clear foundation of absolute truth can limit possible areas of deception. The statement "Both right and wrong; good and evil exist" is an absolute truth. Also, "There is a God" as declared by Antony Flew, is also an absolute truth[31]. Rene Descartes for example stated, *"I think, therefore I am"*[32] which gave a firm basis for reality, rather than the possibility that everything is surreal. Gimbel also states that there are "absolute truths in

---

[28] Gian-Carlo Rota, *The Concept of Mathematical Truth*, The Review of Metaphysics, Vol. 44, No. 3 (Mar., 1991), pp. 483-494 (12 pages) Published By: Philosophy Education Society Inc. https://www.jstor.org/stable/20129055

[29] Kant, Immanuel; *Krit. d. reinen Vernunft* (Critique of Pure Reason), 1st ed., 294 (1781) http://www.commens.org/dictionary/term/mathematical-truth

[30] Gimbel, Steven; *"Are There Absolute Truths in Mathematics?"* (2019) https://www.thegreatcoursesdaily.com/are-there-absolute-truths-in-mathematics/

[31] Flew, Antony; *"There is a God: How the World's Most Notorious Atheist Changed His Mind"*, Harper Collins, (2007)

[32] René Descartes (1596-1650), J. Cottingham, R. Stoothoff, and D. Murdoch. *The Philosophical Writings of Descartes: Volume 1.* Cambridge University Press (2012) (AT VI 32: CSM I 127). (also see: https://1000wordphilosophy.com/2018/11/26/descartes-i-think-therefore-i-am/#_ftn3).

mathematics such that the axioms they are based on remain true"[33]. For further discussions about truth see references at these web pages[34].

WHAT IS DECEPTION?

1 John 2:26 These things I have written to you concerning those who try to deceive you.

The Trojan Horse Legend: Unable to capture the city of Troy after a siege of ten years, the Greek army had resorted to a stratagem. They sailed away and left a huge, hollow, wooden horse as a gift, filled with armed warriors, on the shore of the island. Sinon, a Greek spy who remained behind after the ships departed, deceived and persuaded the Trojans to take the horse in to the city, convincing them that to do so would mysteriously make Troy "invulnerable"[35]. That night, while the Trojans were celebrating their victory and getting drunk, Sinon released the armed Greek troops from the Trojan Horse who then killed the guards and opened the gates to the remaining Greek army who had secretly returned under cover of darkness. Troy was then captured and burned, ending the Trojan War[36]. Similar strategies are employed today in all its variations.

Deceive: to *mislead the mind*; to cause *to believe what is false*, or to disbelieve what is true; while the dictionary defines **deceit:** a *catching* or *ensnaring*. Hence it is the misleading of a person; the leading of another person to believe what is false, or not to believe what is true.

---

[33] Gimbel, Steven, *ibid.*
[34] https://en.wikipedia.org/wiki/Criteria_of_truth   https://iep.utm.edu/truth/ https://www.yourdictionary.com/truth   https://www.skillsyouneed.com/ps/ truthfulness.html
[35] *Trojan Horse*, https://www.britannica.com/topic/Trojan-horse ed. by Adam Augustyn, Encylopaedia Britannica.
[36] *Trojan Horse*, ibid.

MILITARY PLANNING

Psalm 38:12b "Those who seek my hurt speak of destruction, and plan deception all the day long."

In western military appreciation processes, when considering a plan of attack on an enemy, there is always a deception plan to lead the enemy astray. Winston Churchill stated, "In wartime, truth is so precious that she should always be attended by a bodyguard of lies"[37]. The USA even had a Foreign Denial and Deception Committee (FDDC) created by the Reagan Administration to recognize and counter foreign concealment and foreign deception – both military and civilian[38].

Operation Fortitude South was the deception plan associated with Operation Overlord (the actual invasion of Europe by the Allies). This deception plan was designed to deceive the German military high command during World War 2, so that they would place the powerful German tanks opposite Pas de Calais, (along the northern French coast) and not deploy their 15 panzer tank divisions down on the Normandy beaches further south[39]. If these resources had been relocated to defend Normandy, operation overlord could have been jeopardised. The deception was so intricate and multi-faceted that none of the German generals suspected Normandy to be the true objective, even after the landing on D-Day. Deception is a powerful tool in warfare.

---

[37] *"Correct Attributions Or Red Herrings?"* (2013) https://winstonchurchill.org/publications/finest-hour/finest-hour-130/correct-attributions-or-red-herrings/

[38] J Michael Waller, *"US capability to combat foreign deception was shut down, but nobody can explain why"*, (2020), https://www.linkedin.com/pulse/us-capability-combat-foreign-deception-shut-down-nobody-waller

[39] D-Day Invasion of Normandy, see numerous references, including https://www.army.mil/d-day/history.html https://www.britannica.com/event/Normandy-Invasion/Breakout-August-1944 https://www.iwm.org.uk/history/the-10-things-you-need-to-know-about-d-day

A MILITARY ANALYSIS OF DECEPTION

The typology of misperception is described by Whaley, who presented a general theory of deception in a bibliography in 2007[40]. There are two types of perception: Pluperception and Misperception, while pluperception refers to an accurate perception of something, misperception represents a false perception. Whaley writes, "Misperception can be caused by others (Other Induced) or by ourselves (Self-Induced). In any case, whether other-induced or self-induced, the cognitive process is quite similar, if not identical". Whaley describes this taxonomy further: Deception is known as misperception when deliberately caused by others. If, however, misperception is caused unintentionally by others, it is a misrepresentation. This typology of perception was given by the FDDC and listed in the bibliography by Whaley[41]. See Fig. 1 below.

Moore opens an article in the *American Journal of Intelligence* with: "Why are people deceived? What is it about the lie that makes it more attractive than the truth? Why do we often willingly allow ourselves to be fooled? ... We are deceived by others and we are also self-deceived ... – often with deleterious consequences"[42]. Moore is concerned with short term military, national consequences of deception – which can affect thousands of lives – but we are concerned with its eternal consequences.

Moore[43] outlines four general means that deceivers use to influence a "victim's actions and beliefs": Fabrication, Manipulation, Conditioning, and Diversion. Whaley is quoted as defining deception as "any attempt – by words or actions – *intended to distort another person's* or group's *perception of reality*." The ideal deception makes "the victim certain but wrong"[44].

---

[40] Barton Whaley, *Detecting Deception: A Bibliography Of Counterdeception Across Time, Cultures, And Disciplines*, Second Edition, editor: Susan Stratton Aykroyd, Foreign Denial & Deception Committee (FDDC), Washington, DC, March (2006).
[41] Barton Whaley, *ibid.*
[42] David T. Moore, *A Short Primer on Deception and What to Do About It*, American Intelligence Journal, Vol. 32, No. 2 (2015), pp. 3-12 (10 pages), Pub. by: National Military Intelligence Foundation.
[43] David T. Moore, *ibid.*
[44] Barton Whaley, *ibid.*

This is a powerful definition of deception – to distort someone's perception of reality – to lead them to the place where they are so confident of being right – when they are actually misled. How much of our world today is misled as to the basic understanding of the origin of life.

Moore goes on and writes, "Successful deceptions often rely on multiple means ... the repetitive fabrication of false information and the manipulation of true information along with diversionary tactics" was strategic in misleading their military enemy. He also insightfully adds that "If you are going to fool someone, you have to be able to imagine how they're going to interpret and react to your actions"[45]. In other words, our enemy needs to understand how we think so that they can predict how we will react and respond with certain information. Then that information is tailored for the target victim. Moore reminds us that "the effects of successful deception are devastating" and that there are many years of "recorded successful instances of adversarial deception leading to losses of virtue, fortunes, lives and wars"[46].

Kevin Mitnick, 'the world's most famous hacker' and William Simon have written a book titled, "*The Art of Deception*"[47] where they write: "security is not a technology problem – it's a people and management problem"! How interesting that hackers of major corporations refer to the human vulnerability to deception. Mitnick goes on: "The greatest threat to the security of your business assets? That's easy: the social engineer – an unscrupulous magician who has you watching his left hand while with his right he steals your secrets. This character is often so friendly, glib, and obliging that you're grateful for having encountered him". They discuss an example of Stanley Rifkin who used the deceitful skills and techniques (now known as "social engineering") to gain critical account information from the Security Pacific Bank in Los Angeles and obtained a wire transfer of $8 million to his account in Switzerland![48] Didn't need to use a gun or even a computer.

---

[45] David T. Moore, *ibid*.
[46] David T. Moore, ibid.
[47] Kevin D. Mitnick and William L. Simon, "*The Art of Deception, Controlling the Human Element of Security*"; Wiley Publishing Inc. (2002).
[48] Mitnick and Simon; *ibid*.

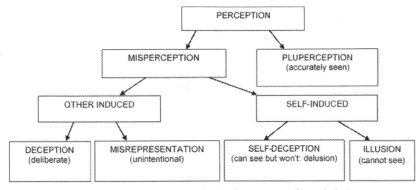

Figure 1: A taxonomy (typology) of Deception (after Whaley)

A traditional definition of deception

To deceive: to intentionally cause to have a false belief that is known or believed to be false. According to this definition, the act of deceiving implies achieving a result, i.e., a false belief[49]. Faveri writes that "Lying and deception are two very closely neighbouring, yet different concepts." He gives a revealing schematic shown below in Figure 2, describing attempted deception, lying and actual deception in his thesis[50].

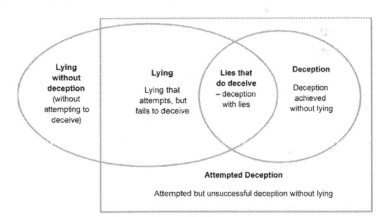

Figure 2: The relationship between lying, deception and attempted deception (after Faveri[51]).

[49] J. E. Mahon, *The Definition of Lying and Deception*, (2007) Stanford Encyclopedia of Philosophy, https://plato.stanford.edu/
[50] Cristiano De Faveri, *Modeling Deception For Cyber Security*, NOVA University Lisbon, (2021) Phd Thesis.
[51] Cristiano De Faveri, *ibid.*

WHO CAN BE DECEIVED?

A Canadian psychologist was quoted in 1991 that the only people not prone to some form of deception were *"those who were clinically insane"*. None of us are immune to deception. We can all fall into some level of deception and believe a lie at times.

Case Studies: Jim Jones and Heavens Gates

Jim Jones in the 1970's deceived 900 people in the People's Temple to believe and trust him, and to follow him in such mad fanaticism that they all committed suicide in November 1978 at the one time in Guyana, a remote country east of Venezuela. Chiu writes for the Rolling Stone[52]:

"It is unfathomable now, as it was then, that more than 900 Americans – members of a San Francisco-based religious group called the Peoples Temple – died after drinking poison at the urging of their leader, the Reverend Jim Jones, in a secluded South American jungle settlement".

How did Jones achieve his aim of destroying all these lives? With multiple lies and deception, about himself, various circumstances, and the people's own blind obedience to him. Be careful what we believe.

A case of mass delusion occurred when 39 members of a UFO cult "Heavens Gates" believed that a spaceship was behind the Hale-Bopp comet in 1997 and committed suicide in order to meet it[53]. It was meant to be a graduation from the "Human Evolutionary Level".

I saw a minor doctrinal error regarding banning dating lead to deception and heartbreak – the international network of 300 churches collapsing in early 1990. The local church in Melbourne no longer exists today. That

---

[52] David Chiu, *Jonestown: 13 Things You Should Know About Cult Massacre*, 29 May 2020, https://www.rollingstone.com/feature/jonestown-13-things-you-should-know-about-cult-massacre-121974/

[53] Wikipedia, *"Heaven's Gate (religious group)"*, https://en.wikipedia.org/wiki/Heaven%27s_Gate_(religious_group)

is the tragedy of allowing deception into the foundation of a church. We need to emphasise the importance of clear biblical balanced doctrine. We need to be vigilant and alert to the devil's cunning musings.

SECTION B: WHY DOES THE DEVIL WANT TO DECEIVE US?

The devil seeks to undermine or hinder God's purposes. He uses disobedience and deception to lead people into rejecting God. The Lord Jesus Christ stripped satan of his power that he had over mankind by His own death and resurrection (Col 2:15; Heb 2:14). If satan cannot destroy us through our sin, he will employ a variety of strategies each with a level of deception associated with it.

Deception: A Primary Strategy of Satan!

Satan is the accuser of the brethren Rev 12:10 and Zech 3:1. His primary strategy is to accuse and deceive the nations so that the strength of his control and dominion over them can increase. As the wickedness of a people increases so does the strength of the satanic grip on them (Matt12:45 and Rom 6:19). This deception takes many forms. The most profound forms of deception begin with denying the existence of God and of the devil himself.

Rev 12:9 So the great dragon was cast out, that serpent of old, called the Devil and Satan, who *deceives the whole world;* he was cast to the earth,

Rev 13:14 And he *deceives* those who dwell on the earth by those signs which he was granted to do in the sight of the beast, …

Rev 18:23b For your merchants were the great men of the earth, for by your sorcery all the nations were *deceived.*

Rev 19:20 … worked signs in his presence, by which he *deceived* those who received the mark of the beast and those who worshiped his image.

Rev 20:3, 7, 8, 10 "he cast him into the bottomless pit, and shut him up, and set a seal on him, so that he should *deceive the nations* no more till the thousand years were finished. ... [7] Satan will be released from his prison [8] and will go out to *deceive the nations* which are in the four corners of the earth ... [10] The devil, who *deceived* them, was cast into the lake of fire ...

Daniel 8:12, 25 and *he cast truth down to the ground*. He did all this and prospered. ... [25] "Through his cunning he shall cause *deceit* to prosper".

Common Lies Used By The Devil To Deceive God's People

"I cannot keep going, I am going to give up before I crack";
"My spouse doesn't love me anymore, this marriage will not work";
"I am too busy to pray";
"I don't have enough time to read the bible";
"I am not good enough for God to use me";
"I really can't run this Bible Study – I must have made a mistake when we started";
"People have hurt me too much, I cannot keep going";
"My leaders have criticised and derided me, I now know I am a failure";
"I am so stressed I cannot relax anymore" (also see Thurman[54]).

SEVEN FORMS OF DECEPTION

1. Lies and Absolute Falsehood is when people unabashedly lie to us

For example, the Gibeonites in

---

[54] Chris Thurman, "*The Lies We Believe*", (1999) and, "*The Lies We Believe Workbook*", (1995), Thomas Nelson Publishers. Also see: Michael Shermer; *Lies We Tell Ourselves: How Deception Leads to Self-Deception*, Scientific American February (2012) https://www.scientificamerican.com/article/lies-we-tell-ourselves/
Matthew Hutson; *Living a Lie: We Deceive Ourselves to Better Deceive Others*, Scientific American April (2017) https://www.scientificamerican.com/article/living-a-lie-we-deceive-ourselves-to-better-deceive-others/

Joshua 9:3, 4, 15 But when the inhabitants of Gibeon heard what Joshua had done to Jericho and Ai, ⁴ they worked craftily, and went and pretended to be ambassadors. … ¹⁴ Then the men of Israel took some of their provisions; but they did not ask counsel of the Lord.

The mistake of the Israelites here is clearly that they did not enquire of the Lord and ask for His counsel or guidance regarding the matter. God will allow us to make mistakes, some costly, while we learn to depend upon Him more regularly (Jam 1:5; Jam 4:2).

2. Incomplete Information when deceit is woven with truth

Laban deceived Jacob into believing that he would give Jacob his second born daughter before the first.

Gen 29:24 – 26 And Laban gave his maid Zilpah to his daughter Leah as a maid. ²⁵ So it came to pass in the morning, that behold, it was Leah. And he said to Laban, "What is this you have done to me? Was it not for Rachel that I served you? Why then have you deceived me?" ²⁶ And Laban said, "It must not be done so in our country, to give the younger before the firstborn."

Jacob here is beginning to reap some of the consequences of his own deceitfulness in obtaining the blessing of Isaac (Gen 27:35). Where if we knowingly deceive others we can also be deceived ourselves (2Tim 3:13).

3. Imbalanced Truth Claims so that the big picture is occluded

Regarding the consumption of food sacrificed to idols, *"Are we free to eat food sacrificed to idols?"* Of course we are, but to state this without qualification is deceitful and misleading. The apostle Paul warns us that as soon as we are told that it is dedicated to an idol, we should not eat of the food lest others stumble because of our liberty.

1Cor 8:7, 11 – 13 But beware lest somehow this liberty of yours become a stumbling block to those who are weak. … [11] And because of your knowledge shall the weak brother perish, for whom Christ died? [12] But when you thus sin against the brethren, and wound their weak conscience, you sin against Christ. [13] Therefore, if food makes my brother stumble, I will never again eat meat, lest I make my brother stumble.

1 Cor 10:23 All things are lawful for me, but not all things are helpful; all things are lawful for me, but not all things edify.

Misusing our liberty can be a bad example to others and is to be avoided at all costs (2Cor 6:3).

4. Doctrinal Confusion: Building a doctrine based upon personal preferences or experiences

"Am I saved by faith or by my works, or both?" Whenever doctrinal issues are to be investigated, we need to address as many scriptures regarding the issue as possible. We should not be swayed by incomplete truths or isolated verses. The bible itself warns to "by the mouth of two or three witnesses every word may be established." (Matt 18:16; also: Deut 17:6; 19:15; 2Cor 13:1; Heb 10:28; 1Tim 5:19). Regarding this question both Paul and James writings need to be considered:

Eph 2:8 – 9 For by grace you have been saved through faith, and that not of yourselves; it is the gift of God, [9] not of works, lest anyone should boast.

James 2:14, 26 What does it profit, my brethren, if someone says he has faith but does not have works? Can faith save him? … [26] For as the body without the spirit is dead, so faith without works is dead also.

Consequently most people agree that it is by faith that we are saved (clearly not by works, Gal 2:21) but that faith will manifest in a changed character resulting in subsequent good deeds (Titus 2:7,14; Titus 3:1, 8, 14).

Similar to doctrinal bias, we can teach as doctrine experiences we have had if we are not diligent to discipline ourselves. "I saw a light, therefore God always communicates in this manner", or "The demon spoke in this manner so it must be true" or "I had this feeling", such a basis will often lead into error, as the bible warns us: *2 Cor 11:14 "For Satan himself transforms himself into angel of light".*

5. Mixture of Truth and Falsehood: where lies and truth merge together

The serpent mixed his own poison in with a command from God and used Eve's carnal desires to agree to listen to his twisted reasoning regarding this commandment. Similar to the common satanic retort, "Go on, yes it might be wrong, but God will forgive you!" Much poison is latent within this temptation that captures the unwary.

Gen 3:1, 4, 5 Now the serpent was more cunning than any beast of the field which the LORD God had made. ... ⁴ Then the serpent said to the woman, "You will not surely die. ⁵ For God knows that in the day you eat of it your eyes will be opened, and you will be like God, knowing good and evil."

6. Truth Quoted Out of Context

Like a deceitful lawyer manipulating phrases of a contract out of context to suit personal gain, we see satan involved in the temptation of Jesus:

Matt 4:5 – 7 Then the devil took him to the holy city and had him stand on the highest point of the temple. ⁶ "If you are the Son of God," he said, "throw yourself down. For it is written: "He will command his angels concerning you, and they will lift you up in their hands, so that you will not strike your foot against a stone."⁷ Jesus answered him, "It is also written: 'Do not put the Lord your God to the test.'"

Here we see that the Lord is not tricked by satan's cunning deceitfulness, but rebukes satan with the word of God!

7. Imitation of Truth

Where copies are made of the authentic in order to mislead. For example, the Egyptian Sorcerers were able to copy some of God's miraculous power, making them appear more powerful than what they really were.

Ex 7:10 – 12 Aaron threw his staff down in front of Pharaoh and his officials, and it became a snake. [11] Pharaoh then summoned wise men and sorcerers, and the Egyptian magicians also did the same things by their secret arts: [12] Each one threw down his staff and it became a snake. But Aaron's staff swallowed up their staffs.

Likewise, false christs and false prophets will imitate the authentic in order to deceive:

Matt 24:4, 5, 23, 24 Jesus answered: "Watch out that no one deceives you. [5] For many will come in my name, claiming, 'I am the Christ', and will deceive many. ... [23] At that time if anyone says to you, 'Look, here is the Christ!' or, 'There he is!' do not believe it. [24] For false christs and false prophets will appear and perform great signs and miracles to deceive even the elect—if that were possible.

Again the apostolic warnings come, "do not be deceived":

2 Thess 2:3 Don't let anyone deceive you in any way, for that day will not come until the rebellion occurs and the man of lawlessness is revealed, the man doomed to destruction.

2 Pet 2:1 But there were also false prophets among the people, just as there will be false teachers among you. They will secretly introduce destructive heresies, even denying the sovereign Lord who bought them.

CONCLUSION

Be aware that our spiritual enemy is trying hard to deceive us. One of satan's major strategies is deception. The consequences of deception are extensive – the damage can be irreparable.

Chapter Review

Types of Truth: Scientific, Historical, Archaeological, Legal, Mathematical and Absolute truth. Deception is the misleading of a person to believe what is false, or not to believe what is true. Some typical examples of common lies used by the devil to deceive God's people were listed. Seven forms of deception: Lies and Falsehood; Incomplete Information; Imbalanced Truth Claims; Doctrinal Confusion; Mixture of Truth and Falsehood; Truth Quoted Out of Context; and Imitation of Truth.

How Do We Respond?

None of us are impervious to various forms of deception. We might be prone to seduction, lust or lies; or to insecurity, pride or jealousy; and the deception they entail.

Let us pray to God that He will reveal any lies currently active in our lives where we are deceived (or in error) to some extent.

Phil 3:15 Therefore let us, as many as are mature, have this mind; and if in anything you think otherwise, God will reveal even this to you!

DECEPTION IS PERVASIVE AND POWERFUL

Avoiding the abyss

"You are a Look-a-Like!" I think it was around Easter 2005 and Helen and I had just arrived at Melbourne Airport prior to catching a bus (down to Philip Island) for our annual national HIM conference. We were waiting in the lobby after picking up our luggage, and a blonde haired middle-aged lady rushed up to us looking quite dishevelled and confused. She said to us in an urgent tone, "Are you the 'real' Brendan and Helen Kirby? I have been told that the real pastors died in the Indian Ocean Tsunami on boxing day while on the coast of Thailand in 2004! I have been told that you are Look-a-Likes, impersonating the real pastors of Hope Church in Adelaide!" I immediately found this quite amusing, but did not show it to the desperate lady. This was obviously an important matter for her to reconcile.

We had a leader in our church leave us in mid-2004 because of confusion and deception over some spiritual matters. This leader had stated to me that I would give up the ministry before the end of 2004, and that a blond European pastor would come and take over the church! He also stated that Helen and I were not the "real" Brendan and Helen but that we were satanic copies sent to infiltrate the church. This was so ridiculous that when this leader first told me of it I didn't think twice about it. But the consternation on the face of the woman at Melbourne Airport told me that the influence of this leader was substantial and that the weight of what they had said carried significant import in her life, to the extent that even the ridiculous had become feasible. We assured this lady that we were indeed the genuine church leaders that we claimed to be!

Deception is a powerful strategy of the enemy of our souls to undermine our lives, ministries and destinies if we are not constantly alert!

SECTION A: ALIGNMENT OF DESIRE

John 8:42, 44 Jesus said to them, "If God were your Father, you would love Me … ⁴⁴ You are of your father the devil, and the desires of your father you want to do. He was a murderer from the beginning, and does not stand in the truth, because there is no truth in him. When he speaks a lie, he speaks from his own resources, for he is a liar and the father of it."

The Lord Jesus Christ here is pointing out that there is an alignment between the desires of the Jews and the desires of the devil. They had been discussing how to murder Jesus and here the Lord is exposing their deceitfulness, and He states that they have aligned their desires with those of the devil.

Instead of aligning their hearts with God, in which case they would operate with a heart of love, and love Jesus, they were deceived into following satan. Why were they deceived and enslaved by satan (John 8: 34)? Because over time they had fallen prey to the system of this world, aligned their values with the world, and had adopted the desires of their spiritual father.

We see here a major clue in avoiding and overcoming deception – being aware of the desires of our hearts – and ensuring we align our heart's values with those of the Kingdom of Heaven!

John 5:19 Then Jesus answered and said to them, "Most assuredly, I say to you, the Son can do nothing of Himself, but what He sees the Father do; for whatever He does, the Son also does in like manner."

Jesus reiterates this clue from back in John 5 where He emphasises that He Himself is aligned perfectly with the desires and values of His Father, therefore it was impossible for Jesus to be deceived or to sin.

ONE OF THE DEVIL'S MOST POWERFUL WEAPONS

2 Cor 4:3, 4 But even if our gospel is veiled, it is veiled to those who are perishing, ⁴ whose minds the god of this age has blinded, who do not believe lest the light of the gospel of the glory of Christ, who is the image of God, should shine on them.

Deception is such a powerful weapon that rejecting the knowledge of God and the gospel of Jesus Christ becomes second nature to those who are blinded by the value system of this world. The idea of a perfect omnipotent Creator who loves them seems ridiculous to somebody who adheres to this world's values of lying, cheating, stealing, surviving and pursuit of pleasure. Hence they are deceived into aligning their values with satan's, and thereby reject the only One who truly loves them and the only way to eternal life. What a great tragedy.

How do we open the minds of those who have been blinded by "the god of this age"? We have to understand ourselves how deception operates, extract any deception we know of operating in our own hearts, and use the truth to begin to challenge and expose the *"straw man"* arguments people cling to.

Prov 21:22 A wise man scales the city of the mighty, and brings down the trusted stronghold.

PEOPLE ARE DECEIVED INTO IGNORING THE SPIRITUAL REALM

In the movie called *"The Matrix"* (1999) a man called Neo finds out that what he thought was real about his life was a complete fabrication in his mind. He realises that his body has been in a cocoon all of his life and he has been experiencing a surreal, dream type world created by a series of master computers. Neo is offered the choice between the blue pill and continuing to live in a synthesized, fictional, computer generated world, or taking the red pill and joining the real world and escaping from the Matrix. Morpheus says to Neo, *"All I am offering you is the truth"*.

As the people in '*The Matrix*' were deceived as to the true nature of reality, so are many in today's society, in that they happily deny or ignore the spiritual realm, thinking that this natural realm is all that matters. Many people in our society would scoff at the idea of spiritual beings such as angels and evil spirits. This deception and ignorance of the spiritual realm is sometimes exposed when the ephemeral nature of life in this natural sphere is confronted and revealed – such as through the death of a loved one, or a tragedy that makes the news. The scripture warns us:

Jer 17:9, 10 "The heart is deceitful above all things, and desperately wicked; who can know it? I, the Lord, search the heart, I test the mind, even to give every man according to his ways, according to the fruit of his doings."

We need to continually search our own hearts for threads of delusion.

Delude: To deceive; to impose upon; to lead away from truth or into error; to mislead the mind or judgement; to beguile. The word 'cheat' is generally applied to deception in bargains; 'delude' to deception in opinions. Satan's promises are deceitfully limited to this world, whereas Jesus contrasts Himself from satan explicitly with the promise of eternal abundant life:

John 10:10 The thief does not come except to steal, and to kill, and to destroy. I have come that they may have life, and that they may have it more abundantly.

Once Truth Is Agreed Upon, False Statements Must Be Seen As False

Once we agree upon a given set of axioms, then we immediately exclude an infinite number of other answers which are all wrong. There is only one right answer (within this chosen mathematical domain).

The statement, *"What is true for you, is true for you; and what is true for me, is true for me",* will open us to deception if we extend this logic too an extreme. It is true in that some truth can be a personal experience – some of the feelings and emotional responses we experience others will never experience, and vice versa, as each person responds to life differently.

The statement *"murder is a crime"* is true for all human beings and is not subject to personal evaluation such as *"Is it true for me or not?".*

IS THERE A GOD, OR DID THE UNIVERSE AND LIFE 'JUST HAPPEN'?

Prov 3: 19 The Lord by wisdom founded the earth; by understanding He established the heavens

Two major events that remain inexplicable from a naturalistic viewpoint, are the beginning of the universe (at a particular point in time about 13.8Gyrs ago) and the formation of the first replicating life form (the origin of life). Both these facts point clearly to a divine designer.

Norman Geisler writes regarding the existence of God: 'At one level, it is a truth we can't not know. At another level, it is *a truth people repeatedly deny*'[55]. Many of us go through life, not really pursuing what is true. Pirsig states: *'The truth knocks at the door, you say "Go away I'm looking for the truth", so truth goes away'*[56]. A number of academics promulgate

[55] Geisler, Norman L.; *'Baker Encyclopaedia of Christian Apologetics'* (1998). Baker Reference Library, Baker Academic.
[56] Pirsig, Robert M.; *'Zen and the Art of Motorcycle Maintenance: An Inquiry Into Values'*, (2006), Harper Torch.

alternatives as proven fact, when it is indeed far from it. Philip Johnson questions whether *"Scientific investigation is driven by the evidence or driven by preconceived conclusions?"*[57].

Richard Dawkins, the prominent Oxford geneticist, states "Biology is the study of complicated things that give *the appearance of having been designed for a purpose*"[58]. Sir Francis Crick, co-discoverer of the structure of the DNA molecule: "Biologists must constantly keep in mind that what they see *was not designed, but rather evolved*"[59]. This gives the impression of imposing upon oneself to believe a certain model, in spite of overwhelming evidence to the contrary. Dawkins goes on to reveal his bias, "It is absolutely safe to say that, if you meet somebody who claims not to believe in evolution, that person is ignorant, stupid, or insane"[60].

God's Existence provides the Foundation for Good and Evil, Right and Wrong

Dawkins has concluded that *"life has no design, no purpose, no evil and no good, nothing but blind pitiless indifference"*, as a natural consequence of life evolving[61]. The whole concept of good and evil can only come from our Creator. There can be no right or wrong without a personal, moral Creator. Human beings have no authority to dictate right or wrong to

[57] Johnson, Philip E.; '*The Wedge of Truth: Splitting the Foundations of Naturalism*', (2002), Inter Varsity Press.

[58] Dawkins, Richard; "*The Blind Watchmaker: Why the Evidence of Evolution Reveals a Universe Without Design*", (1996), Turtleback Books.

[59] Crick, Francis; "*Biologists must constantly keep in mind that what they see was not designed, but rather evolved.*" Quoted from 'What Mad Pursuit: A Personal View of Scientific Discovery' (1990), p138, Basic Books.

[60] Dawkins, R. April 9, 1989. *Book Review of Donald Johanson and Maitland Edey's Blueprint.* The New York Times. Section 7, 34.

[61] Scheff, Liam, 2007. *The Dawkins Delusion*. Salvo. 2:94. Quoted by Evolution's Evangelists, May 01, 2008 https://www.icr.org/article/evolutions-evangelists

one another – only a Higher Being can do that. Remember a computer has no knowledge of good or evil, love or hate, or of pleasure or suffering. To deny the existence of true and false, or of right and wrong will open a person up to living with contradictions between their values and their lifestyle.

Even the great philosopher and atheist Bertrand Russell wrestled with his denial that God existed and admitted in a letter to Lady Otto: "Even when one feels nearest to other people, something in one seems obstinately *to belong to God*, and to refuse to enter into any earthly communion – at least that is how I should express it if I thought there was a God"[62].

Prov 8: 27, 28 – 30a When He prepared the heavens, I was there, when He drew a circle on the face of the deep, [28] When He established the clouds above, when He strengthened the fountains of the deep, [29] when He assigned to the sea its limit, so that the waters would not transgress His command, when He marked out the foundations of the earth, [30] Then I was beside Him as a master craftsman; …

SECTION B: DOES DNA POINT TO THE EXISTENCE OF GOD?

Ps 139: 13,14 For You formed my inward parts; You covered me in my mother's womb. [14] I will praise You, for I am fearfully and wonderfully made; marvelous are Your works, and that my soul knows very well.

Are Dawkins and Crick wilfully denying evidence of design? If we objectively observe the beauty and functionality of irreducibly complex organisms it seems at least reasonable that the "appearance of design" might have some intentionality behind it. What if we look at the complexity inside the nucleus of every single cell in a human body? We would see the most complex molecule in the universe! It's known as DNA.

---

[62] Russell, Bertrand and Foot, Michael; *Autobiography of Bertrand Russell*, 11ᵗʰ Aug 1918, page 320, (1998), published by Routledge.

Helmenstine[63] writes that DNA is the nucleic acid that codes for genetic information. It codes the information for all of the proteins that make up an organism. Two of the DNA facts that Helmenstine notes are:

If you put all the DNA molecules in your body end to end, the DNA would reach from the Earth to the Sun and back over 100 times.

If you could type at a rate of 60 words per minute, for eight hours a day, 7 days a week, it would take approximately 50 years to type out all of the information within the human genome.

That's amazing! This molecule is in every cell in our body governing protein formation and cell replication every second we are alive!

Just for context, Sender and his team of the Weizmann Institute of Science write that the number of cells in the human body is averaged at around 30 trillion;[64] and Mann estimates that the number of different proteins in the human body (known as the "human proteome") is between 80 thousand and 400 thousand[65]. Starr quotes the work by Sender and Milo and states that the average human body is forming about 4 million new cells every second[66]. Their creation is a continuous process, and a single protein chain can have 10-15 amino acids added to it per second via the protein formation process (outlined in more detail in this YouTube video of protein formation[67]).

---

[63] Anne Marie Helmenstine, *DNA Definition and Structure, What Is DNA?*, Updated on Jan 08, 2018, https://www.thoughtco.com/definition-of-dna-and-structure-604433

[64] Sender R, Fuchs S, Milo R (2016) *Revised Estimates for the Number of Human and Bacteria Cells in the Body*. PLoS Biol 14(8): e1002533. https://doi.org/10.1371/journal.pbio.1002533

[65] Matthias Mann, *The Protein Puzzle*, Max Planck Research 3 (17) page 54 https://www.mpg.de/11447687/W003_Biology_medicine_054-059.pdf

[66] Michelle Starr, *Your Body Makes 3.8 Million Cells Every Second. Most of Them Are Blood*, 23 Jan 2021 https://www.sciencealert.com/your-body-makes-4-million-cells-a-second-and-most-of-them-are-blood

[67] Please feel free to look up the amazing and astonishing video of protein formation: https://www.youtube.com/watch?v=gG7uCskUOrA

The real problem is when we lose a love for the truth

When a person denies what is clearly true, deception begins to take a hold of their heart. Once a person becomes used to the deception, it spreads into other areas of their lives. At one time Jesus rebuked his disciples because they did not know what spirit they were of. This shows us it is quite easy for us to be misled by the promptings of other spirits apart from the Holy Spirit:

Luke 9:51 – 56 And when His disciples James and John saw this, they said, "Lord, do You want us to command fire to come down from heaven and consume them, just as Elijah did?" But He turned and rebuked them, and said, "You do not know what manner of spirit you are of. For the Son of Man did not come to destroy men's lives but to save them."

The power of deception: We can choose to believe whatever we want to believe. People can believe in almost anything. This 'blind choice' can overrule what is true. For example, there are still people who are members of the Flat Earth Society. The devil is looking for those whom he can deceive:

1Pet 5:8, 9 Be sober, be vigilant; because your adversary the devil walks about like a roaring lion, seeking whom he may devour. ⁹ Resist him, steadfast in the faith …

The value of truth is undermined nowadays. Few people pursue or care about the truth, and many are content with a simplistic self-satisfied view of life: "eating and drinking; buying and selling, marrying and giving in marriage".

DETECTING DECEPTION: CAN WE TELL IF SOMEONE IS LYING?

There is an activity run by Psychologist Dr Zoe Walkington at The Open University in the UK. They rank how well a person thinks they can tell if someone is lying before starting the test. Dr Zoe provides 8 cases where the person needs to decide which of the 8 are lying[68]. I failed this test, I got 2/8 – worse than a monkey would score (statistically speaking)! So I recommend you give it a go!

Most people perform around chance level in this task. One reason we are so poor at discerning who is lying, is the tendency to rely on cues that are not actually useful in detecting deception. When a person looks away (gaze aversion), or fidgets or self-grooms, these types of behaviours do not correlate with deceit[69]. Police officers also perform at around the chance level, even when evaluating real criminals in high stake situations[70]. Confidence and accuracy do not correlate, therefore a person's confidence is not an accurate reflection of their capability to discern deceit[71].

Ekman laments, "When people lie to one another, much damage is done in relationships. Once you trust some one who is deceitful, you may have problems discerning the truth"[72]. He discusses two primary types of lies: Concealing lies (withholding some information) and Falsifying lies (presenting false information as if it were true) and mentions 4 other ways of lying. He has found that avoiding punishment is the primary motivator for lying. Tragically he writes that "deception is a central characteristic of life. *Most (if not all) human relationships involve some form of deceit, or at least the possibility of it.*"[73].

---

[68] Zoe Walkington, *Detecting Deception, Some people are lying to you. Others are telling the truth. Can you tell which is which?* The Open University in the UK, https://learning.elucidat.com/course/5e15ef4ca5d25-5e15f0b95185a

[69] Bond, Charles; Levine, Timothy and Hartwig, Maria, *New Findings in Non-Verbal Lie Detection*, (2014). https://www.researchgate.net/publication/278312651_New_Findings_in_Non-Verbal_Lie_Detection

[70] Aldert Vrij and Samantha Mann, *Telling and detecting lies in a high-stake situation: the case of a convicted murderer*, Journ. Applied Cognitive Psychology, Volume15, Issue2, March/April 2001, Pages 187-203.

[71] Aldert Vrij, *ibid.*

[72] Paul Ekman, *What Is A Lie?* https://www.paulekman.com/deception/ accessed 6th April 2022. Also see: Dina Gerdeman, *How To Deceive Others With Truthful Statements (It's Called 'Paltering,' And It's Risky)*, Dec (2016) https://www.forbes.com/sites/hbsworkingknowledge /2016/12/05/how-to-deceive-others-with-truthful-statements-its-called-paltering-and-its-risky/?sh=792a50f0577a

[73] Paul Ekman, *ibid.*

THE PROBLEM: WE THINK WE CAN
TELL WHEN SOMEONE IS LYING

"I promise I will return the money to you pastor, you can rely on me. Next Sunday I will be here with $50. Not a problem. Thank you so much for trusting me pastor, I really appreciate your kindness. You are a kind man. You have helped me so much. I will see you next Sunday!" Of course I never saw them again.

"Brendan, I know I let you down, I know I should not have used the $1500 you lent to me for my airfare back to Malaysia to indulge myself in the Brisbane casino. But I really need another $300 to get home. I promise I will repay you Brendan! I really need your help. I promise I will repay the $1800 completely – you can rely on me. I really appreciate you Brendan, you are such a good guy." Needless to say I never saw my $1800 again. In this particular case I drove the young Malaysian man to Melbourne airport to see him depart (finally) for his own country. We were having a relaxing coffee together at the airport lounge, and he said he was going to the men's room. He stood up and walked away from the table. After he had walked away, this intense grief came over me, and I began crying quite profusely, as if my tears were a form of intercessory prayer for this man – who was most likely going back to his gang and a life of crime. The tears included a sense of despair as well – as if his future was not going to go well, and not even the Spirit of God reaching out to him could restrain him. God's love for His lost sheep is quite incredible. Suddenly the tears stopped, I regained my composure, he then came back to the table and we continued our conversation as if nothing had happened.

We need God's wisdom when people are
telling us their side of their story

Prov 18:17 "The first one to plead his cause seems right, until his neighbor comes and examines him".

When conversing with those I do not know well, I find myself slipping into a default mode where I want to trust them. This is because I naturally think that I can tell when people are lying to me – so that means I can choose to trust them (because they are not lying). But I have often proved myself wrong – to my own dismay of lowering the level of cash in my wallet (as above)! Nowadays I try to remind myself that *I cannot tell if people are lying*. I have to train myself to defer any decision until I talk to other people and gather more data or evidence. This is a big lesson in avoiding being deceived or even just misled by those who appear all too sincere.

Case Study of a Liar

A classic example is that of Craig Thomson who was the national secretary of the Health Services Union from 2002 until 2007 when he was elected as a federal MP (a member of the House of Representatives). Misuse of the union's funds was identified in 2008 by external auditors. Later, tax specialists were tasked to investigate potential inappropriate use of the union's credit card. Ewart wrote that "Thomson denied all wrongdoing and stated that an independent audit had not identified any inappropriate use of the card"[74]. In front of parliament in 2012 Thomson affirmed his own innocence, stated that others could have used his credit card, named other people who were attempting to discredit him, and claimed he was being set up. He was in tears as he pled his own innocence and pointed at Tony Abbot as "releasing the lynch mob" and then at the press emotionally stating "you have fanned" the flames of accusation. Ewart stated that even the most cynical would have been moved by this maudlin display, and then begin to trust Thomson[75].

Nevertheless, Thomson was later found guilty in 2014 (after lying fervently about his innocence for 4 years) of 65 charges of fraud and theft, and sentenced to 12 months jail. His behavior continued on this line of deceit until even recently (2021) where he was convicted of credit card fraud of $2M[76].

---

[74] Heather Ewart, "*Craig Thomson outlines 'set up' in HSU scandal*", Posted Mon 21 May 2012, http://www.abc.net.au/7.30/content/2012/s3507737.htm

[75] Heather Ewart, *ibid.*

[76] Craig Thomson (politician), https://en.wikipedia.org/wiki/Craig_Thomson_(politician)

WE CANNOT TELL WHEN SOMEONE IS LYING

Seigel[77] quotes psychologist Maria Hartwig: "The mistakes of lie detection are costly to society and people victimised by misjudgments, … *The stakes are really high.*" Seigel cites work by DePaulo and Bond (of TCU) who reviewed "206 studies involving 24,483 observers judging the veracity of 6,651 communications by 4,435 individuals. Neither law enforcement experts nor student volunteers were able to pick true from false statements better than 54% of the time!" Amazing.

If even seasoned police officers struggle to discern if someone is lying[78], how much more should we be wise and discerning, and wait for confirmation before committing to trust one side of an account. If in doubt, ask more questions and obtain more information.

Paul Ekman writes that "The answer from 20 years of research is that people have not been very accurate in judging when someone is lying"[79]. Ekman quotes 3 studies of *professional lie catchers* (customs officials, federal law enforcement officers and police officers) which found that they could not detect a lie any better than untrained college students! He does quote a study were secret service officers performed better than average in detecting liars – but these were an unusual group[80].

Vrij *et al.* have written a review on "Reading Lies: Nonverbal Communication and Deception" and show that "the nonverbal cues to deceit discovered to date are *faint and unreliable* and that people are mediocre lie catchers when they pay attention to behavior"[81]. Also they found that "people *overestimate*

---

[77] Jessica Seigel, *'Can you tell when someone is lying?'*, https://www.bbc.com/future/article/20210401-how-to-tell-when-someone-is-lying, (2021).

[78] Jessica Seigel, *ibid.*

[79] Paul Ekman, *Who Can Catch Liars?* https://www.paulekman.com/blog/who-can-catch-liars/ accessed 6th April 2022.

[80] Paul Ekman, *ibid.*

[81] Aldert Vrij, Maria Hartwig, and Pär Anders Granhag, *Reading Lies: Nonverbal Communication and Deception*, Annual Review of Psychology, Vol. 70 (2019) page 295. https://www.annualreviews.org/doi/10.1146/annurev-psych-010418-103135

the relationship between nonverbal behavior and deception and assume many relationships that are actually *untrue* (stereotypes)!"

Seigel writes[82] that Tankleff seemed too calm after finding his mother stabbed to death and his father mortally bludgeoned. Authorities didn't believe his claims of innocence, and he spent 17 years in prison for the murders. In another case, detectives thought that Deskovic seemed too distraught and too eager to help after his friend was found strangled. He was also judged to be lying and served nearly 16 years for the crime. One man was not upset enough. The other was too upset. Hartwig states[83] that they were victims of a pervasive misconception: that *"you can spot a liar by the way they act"*.

Steinhilber[84] writes that "60 percent of people can't go 10 minutes without lying at least once." Garrett *et al.* show that "the extent to which participants engage in self-serving dishonesty increases with repetition"[85] and that "what begins as small acts of dishonesty can escalate into larger transgressions". Baker *et al.* state that a high "EI (Emotional Intelligence) was associated with *overconfidence* in assessing the sincerity of the pleas and greater self-reported sympathetic feelings to deceptive targets (enhanced gullibility)."[86] Leading to their finding that: "features of EI, and subsequent decision-making processes, paradoxically may impair one's ability to detect deceit." So if we are high in EI then beware of overconfidence, because we can still be deceived.

---

[82] Jessica Seigel, *ibid.*

[83] Aldert Vrij, Maria Hartwig, and Pär Anders Granhag, *ibid.*

[84] Brianna Steinhilber, *How to tell if someone is lying to you, according to researchers* (2017) https://www.nbcnews.com/better/amp/ncna786326

[85] Neil Garrett, Stephanie C Lazzaro, Dan Ariely and Tali Sharot, *The brain adapts to dishonesty*, Nature Neuroscience vol. 19, page1727 (2016). https://www.nature.com/articles/nn.4426

[86] Alysha Baker, Leanne ten Brinke, Stephen Porter *Will get fooled again: Emotionally intelligent people are easily duped by high-stakes deceivers*, (2013) Legal and Criminological Psychology Vol 18 page 300. https://bpspsychub.onlinelibrary.wiley.com/doi/10.1111/j.2044-8333.2012.02054.x

Note that I have only touched on a huge research area of criminology and do not claim to be an expert (there is much more material that I have not referenced). But I have provided some references to establish that the research is clearly revealing the difficulty in detection of deceit in human relationships. Therefore the advice is not to trust someone simply based upon their word alone. Be resolute in obtaining the other side of the story and confirming evidence. As Moore would recommend: "Look for incongruities".

CONCLUSION

Today we want to encourage you to believe in the spiritual realm! We need to have a strong faith in God that does not waver under various circumstances. Be aware that satan is the god of this world (2Cor 4:4; 1John 5:19), he is the father of lies and everything he does flows from a lie (John 8:44). Therefore, we should expect this world to be full of deception and lies. We will often be deceived if we think we can discern on face value whether other people are lying to us. Remember that each of us are susceptible to deception, especially if we assume we are above it.

Chapter Review

Protection from deception can be increased when we align our desires with those of the Lord.

Deception is one of the devil's most powerful weapons and causes great eternal loss of life.

People are deceived into ignoring the spiritual realm or repudiating its existence.

Once truth is agreed upon, false statements need to be seen as false.

Life and the universe cannot 'just happen'. Logically, every contingent effect must have a cause.

God's existence provides the foundation for justice, good and evil, right and wrong.

The incredible complexity of DNA clearly points to the existence of a Transcendent Designer.

Detecting deception is not simple. The problem is that we think we can tell when someone is lying.

We need God's wisdom when people are telling us their side of their story. Basically (most of the time) we cannot tell when someone is lying.

How Do We Respond?

Be alert. Watch and pray. Be wary of the fear that conspiracy theories can generate. Some may be true – many may not be. Waves of misinformation and conjecture are being unleashed upon nations and we need to overcome these waves of deception and fear.

Be ready for the storm that is coming to test all of us – whether our house is built upon the Rock of the teachings of Jesus Christ or upon the Sand of wilful ignorance.

We must stand strong in our faith in Jesus Christ!

Actively resist complacency – choose to be active in our faith!

Put our faith into action – overcome the devil's lies, temptations and promises!

HOW DOES A PERSON BECOME DECEIVED?

A pictorial description

Job 28:27, 28 Then He saw wisdom and declared it; He prepared it, indeed, He searched it out. [28] *And to man He said, 'Behold, the fear of the Lord, that is wisdom, and to depart from evil is understanding.'"*

I turned frantically to the left and fervently to the right – there was nothing to grab a hold of. I was on the edge of a cliff – more technically the edge of the Bluff at Barwon Heads in Victoria. The four of us siblings were walking precipitously along this ledge and I began to slip on the loose pebbles. I was probably only 5 years of age, and my brothers maybe 10 and 11; Carmel 12. I looked down at the rocks and waves crashing on them about 60m below. I assessed my situation as grave when I saw no weeds or branches to reach out to and stop my slide downwards. In the next half second I realised I was going to die and there really was nothing to stop my fall. Before I could begin to panic and feel adrenaline kick in for the short remainder of my life – I saw an outstretched hand. It was my brother Paul's. Miraculously he had turned back and reacted phenomenally fast to step back and quietly reach out his hand in a fraction of a second. I reached up – grabbed his hand – he pulled me up onto the safety of the ledge – and we kept walking as if nothing had happened. We never spoke about it. Michael and Carmel who were just in front of us did not even see that death defying episode. Years later I would think about that event – and it really dawned on me that I should have died without my brother's outstretched hand. If we think we can go through life on our own we really do deceive ourselves. We need each other. We are designed to work best together. Isolation should never be an option (Prov 18:1).

Our life consists of the decisions we make

Wise decision making should therefore be of the highest priority in our lives. Hence we are encouraging the pursuit of wisdom. But deception is a major stumbling block to wise decision making and leads directly into foolishness. Therefore exposing deception and revealing its roots and causes should be of the utmost importance.

In order to describe some of the roots of deception more clearly we have drawn up a schematic of the foundation and primary causes of deception – this is in parallel with the architecture of wisdom where we showed from scripture the importance of the fear of the Lord and Christ Crucified, followed by a selection of 7 pillars from proverbs.

The different levels in the architecture of deception will be briefly outlined first, with explanations of their biblical basis provided in detail in Appendix B.

Level 1: Rebellion, Unbelief and Self-Will

Rebellion can be described as choosing what I want (so self-will is included on this level for more clarity) and is a rejection of the Lord and His ways. Unbelief is refusing to believe what is clearly revealed. Rebellion and unbelief are the foundation or source of sin, and lead to disobedience. These elements overlap each other significantly and are fundamental in the disconnection from our Creator. The author of the book of Hebrews links rebellion to sin, and unbelief to disobedience:

Heb 3:16 – 19 For who, having heard, rebelled? Indeed, was it not all who came out of Egypt, led by Moses? ¹⁷ Now with whom was He angry forty years? Was it not with those who sinned, whose corpses fell in the wilderness? ¹⁸ And to whom did He swear that they would not enter His rest, but to those who did not obey? ¹⁹ So we see that they could not enter in because of unbelief.

Level 2: Sin, Disobedience and Lawlessness

The rebellion and unbelief directly lead to sin and disobedience. All sin is lawlessness (1John 3:4) so we have included the latter on this level. Sin promises short term pleasure and selfish gain but leads to heartache and disappointment (Gal 6:7).

Level 3: Pride, Charm, Hypocrisy and Lies

Practising pride, charm, hypocrisy and lying lead directly into increasing levels of deception. What this indicates is that when we see these behaviours (or four elements) being practised we know that there will concomitantly be some deception operating in the person.

Level 4: Fear, Selfish-Ambition, Seduction and Partiality

Once a person has been deceived to some extent, then other behaviours emerge that are consistent with somebody who is already deceived; namely: fear (linked with insecurity), selfish ambition (linked with jealousy), seduction (linked with lust) and partiality (linked with man's approval). These four attributes are not necessarily causative (but can be) of deception as the above elements in level 3 – they are mainly the consequences of an initial certain level of deception.

The four above behaviours are all deceitful activities which lead others into deception, as well as the person operating in these behaviours.

Level 5: Trusting In Vain, Futile Things (Lies, Man, Beauty, Riches)

Also inserted into the deception architecture are some aspects of trusting in Lies, Man, Riches, Beauty etc. If we trust in ephemeral, futile things to provide eternal security we will be disappointed, and hence that trust has led many into some level of deception:

Job 15:31 Let him not trust in futile things, *deceiving himself*, for futility will be his reward.

Referring to the Chaldeans who lived in Babylon, Isaiah wrote to those who trusted in their own wickedness:

Isaiah 47:10 "For you have *trusted in your wickedness*; you have said, 'No one sees me'; your wisdom and your knowledge have *warped* you; and you have said in your heart, 'I am, and there is no one else besides me.'

Level 6: Rejection of the knowledge of God and the subsequent curse of rejection

Romans 1 outlines the increasing depravity of those who reject the knowledge of God and suppress the truth. This leads into futile thinking and a darkening of their foolish hearts (Rom 1:21). Once we reject God, we cut off our acceptance into His family and we become spiritual orphans suffering from the uncertainty of our origins and the confusion of rejection – causing us to look for "acceptance" in all the wrong places.

A SPIRITUAL ARCHITECTURE FOR DECEPTION!

ANTICHRIST IS A LIAR Satan's Lies					
Trust in Lies	Trust in Man	Trust in Beauty	Trust in Riches	Reject the knowledge of God	Curse of Rejection
FEAR and Insecurity	**SELFISH AMBITION** and Jealousy		**SEDUCTION** and Lust		**PARTIALITY** and Man's Approval
PRIDE	**CHARM**		**LIES**		**HYPOCRISY**
SIN		**DISOBEDIENCE**		**LAWLESSNESS**	
REBELLION		**UNBELIEF**		**SELF-WILL**	

Chart 1: A proposed spiritual architecture outlining the key components of deception. The promises of sin if embraced, believed and practised produce deception. The processes are elucidated in Chart 2 below.

Level 7: Anti-Christ and Satan's Lies

The capstone in this architecture of deception consists of "Anti-Christ". Since Christ Crucified is the pinnacle of God's wisdom and truth, the opposite is the depth of deception, which is to deny that Jesus is the Christ, the Son of God:

1John 2:22 Who is a **liar** but he who denies that Jesus is the Christ? He is **antichrist** who denies the Father and the Son.

*2John 1:7 For many **deceivers** have gone out into the world who do not confess Jesus Christ as coming in the flesh. This is a **deceiver** and an **antichrist**.*

The rejection of Jesus Christ is from the spirit of antichrist and this deception will lead us away from our only source of salvation and therefore is a highly dangerous lie of the enemy.

CONCLUSION: *PROCESSES BEHIND DECEPTION*

As with the Architecture of Wisdom, the Architecture of Deception is not meant to be a complete description of the causes of deception, but is to present to the reader a good starting point to describe how deception operates. If we can expose and overcome all of the above factors in our own personal lives, then we will be well on the way to living in a higher level of truth and integrity before God. The levels shown in Chart 1 provide a basis for other deceitful activities that cause us to trust in what we can gain from embracing them. Chart 2 below gives a flow chart that provides more detail about the processes behind deception.

Without God the experience of the human condition suffers from deep insecurity and rejection. All of us are plagued with differing degrees of insecurity and rejection as a result of our sin and separation from God. These can be ameliorated with a revelation of the acceptance, love and security we have in Jesus Christ.

Chapter Review

The enemy of wisdom is deception. If we are deceived then our values change depending upon the type of deception. Consequently our decision making will change. Deception takes root and we think we are wise when in reality others can see we are being foolish. Therefore we must be diligent to expose and uproot all types of deception from our lives and any tendencies we might have to deceive others.

How Do We Respond?

The architecture of deception is provided as a tool for reflection and self-analysis to expose areas in our lives where weaknesses will almost certainly be doorways for different forms of deception.

For example – ask the Lord to search our hearts for any hidden sin:

1 John 1:8 If we say that we have no sin, we deceive ourselves, and the truth is not in us.

Have we trusted in people who hold to errant values that conflict with the Word of God? If we are attuned to their advice then we will often be led astray:

2 Pet 2:3 By covetousness they will exploit you with deceptive words; for a long time their judgment has not been idle, and their destruction does not slumber.

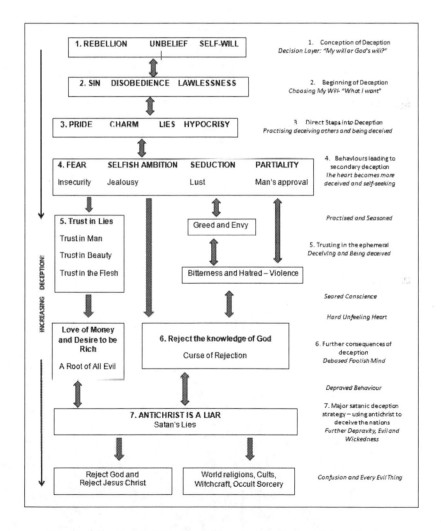

Chart 2: More Detailed Flow Chart Revealing the Processes Behind Deception
Note: Feedback arrows to increase the deception

10

HOW DO WE ESCAPE AND OVERCOME DECEPTION?

Some strategies

I used to live with my parents in Lower Plenty in Melbourne while I was a post-graduate student at Melbourne University. My parents had landscaped the land next to our house so that it had a garden with a small creek with a pond at its base and a water-pump recycling the water from the pond to the outlet at the top of the creek. The water flow was sufficient to keep some plants and a few small goldfish alive in this pond. One pleasant feature of this pond was that it picked up some frogs that made it their home.

One summer our neighbours crossed the road and came over for a cup of tea with mum one afternoon. I said to them that the "*knee-dep; knee-dep*" that we could hear coming rhythmically in time in a remarkably repeatable fashion from the pond was an "electronic frog" that we used to fool people into believing that it was a real frog! This was a plausible idea because the volume, pitch and duration of the "*knee-dep*" and the period of time between them were almost identical so that it really did sound like a mechanical device with periodic repetitions. I thought it was a joke, that my "lie" would be exposed with their disbelief that an electronic frog could emulate a real frog so accurately – and my mother sat there bemused knowing that I was just joking – because the sound was coming from a real frog, and my family all knew that.

The surprise was that the neighbour was so fully convinced by my first discourse of rhetoric about the "electronic frog" and how we used it to trick other people, that when I later revealed the truth that it actually was a "real frog" she completely disbelieved me and rejected what I said, repeating what I had said! I was amazed. Here I was, confessing my lie to her, yet she refused to believe me. So convinced was she that the sound was coming from an electronic frog that there was nothing I could say to dissuade her! My mother appropriately reproved me later for misleading her. Some years later the neighbour would still pass comments about our "electronic frog". My mother could not believe the power of the deception that I had inadvertently cast upon her.

Isaiah 19:13, 14 The princes of Zoan have become fools; the princes of Noph are deceived; they have also deluded Egypt, those who are the mainstay of its tribes. ¹⁴ The Lord has mingled a perverse spirit in her midst; and they have caused Egypt to err in all her work, as a drunken man staggers in his vomit.

Isaiah warns the princes and counsellors of Pharaoh that if they trust in idols then they will be deceived and cause Egypt to err. For church leaders it is incumbent upon them to cast off any source of deception in their own lives and be circumspect as to who they listen to and trust. Paul the apostle exhorts us to choose faithful and proven people to be our co-labourers and confidants (2Tim 2:2, Phil 2:22, 1Tim 3:10 and 2Cor 8:22).

SECTION A: BASIC LIES THAT CAUSE CONFUSION AND DECEPTION WHICH CAUSE DAMAGE

Lutzer[87] describes (and discusses in detail in his book) ten common lies about God:

---

[87] Erwin W. Lutzer *"Ten Lies About God, and how you might already be deceived"* Word Publishing, Nashville (2000).

God is whatever we want Him to be;
Many paths lead into God's presence;
God is more tolerant than He used to be;
God has never personally suffered;
God is obligated to save followers of other religions;
God takes no responsibility for natural disasters;
God does not know our decisions before we make them;
The Fall of Adam and Eve ruined God's plan;
We must choose between God's pleasures and our own;
God helps those who help themselves.

We can add to this list with the following:

I do not think that the bible is the only word of God (2Tim 3:16, 17). Unfortunately some people pick and choose what they want to believe about God, to their own peril.

Only some parts of the bible are inspired (2Pet 1:21). I heard a famous speaker at a seminar in Melbourne at Monash University claim he did not believe the Gospel of John was from God.

I have to do a theology degree to serve God (1Tim 3:1). A traditional way of thinking but should not limit us.

I can have sin in my life and I know that God still loves me. (James 1:15,16; James 4:4). Friendship with the world makes us an enemy of God.

I can allow myself to do the wrong thing and God will forgive me (Gal 6:7). Do not be deceived, God is not mocked, whatever we sow, we shall reap.

My friends do not affect me, I am a strong Christian (1Cor 15:33). Our friends will drag us down spiritually.

I gave my heart to the Lord, now I am saved, once saved I am always saved (Heb 6:4-6; Col 1:23; Heb 10:26). I can be confident in my salvation if I continue to obey the Lord.

I do not need to attend church – I can get along fine by myself (Prov 18:1, Heb 10:25). Some justify their self-isolation by the hurt they've experienced, but we must forgive others.

I can be a friend of the world, and God still approves of me (James 4:4), No we become God's enemy.

I do not need to pray (1Thess 5:17). This is not a cognitive deception, our actions reveal what we truly believe, i.e. that we do not actually pray.

More detailed studies of "*Lies that we Believe*" are didactically given by Dr Chris Thurman[88].

Why Do People Practise Deceit?

Col 2:4 I say this in order that no one may delude (or deceive) you with plausible arguments.

A delusion is the result of persuading someone that something false is actually true; or that something true is false. People practise deceit, charm and bring others into some level of deception regarding what is true for a variety of reasons. All of these have a selfish root:
to seduce or attract for personal gain (lust of the flesh);
to gain a higher position (envy);
to achieve greater recognition and fame (selfish ambition);
to garner another's attention out of a sense of personal competition (jealousy);
to earn more money (love of money);
to grow in power (Jezebel: control, domination, manipulation, intimidation);
to have man's approval (peers, especially for young people).

---

[88] Chris Thurman, "*The Lies We Believe*", (1999), Thomas Nelson Publishers; and Chris Thurman, "*The Lies We Believe Workbook*", (1995), Thomas Nelson Publishers.

Someone Will Betray Our Love and Trust

King David experienced betrayal by his own sons Amnon (who raped his daughter Tamar), Absalom (who attempted to usurp the kingdom through outright rebellion), and Adonijah (who promoted himself as king dismissing his father's intentions). He was particularly heartbroken over the demise of Absalom (2Sam 19) despite Absalom's overt murderous intentions. Even David's loyal army general Joab betrayed him in the end (1King 1). Through these experiences of betrayal David was able to write explicitly about the hidden treachery of close friends (also experienced by the Messiah):

Psalm 41:9 Even my own familiar friend in whom I trusted, who ate my bread, has lifted up his heel against me.

Psalm 55:21 The words of his mouth were smoother than butter, but war was in his heart; his words were softer than oil, yet they were drawn swords.

Most (probably all) of us will experience some form of betrayal in our lives. For some, it might be the realisation that a close friend was deceitful in the way that they conducted the friendship. Some friendly people look like they genuinely care about others but their outgoing personality is tainted with selfish agendas, and these agendas lead them to eventually betray their own stated values. Their friends suddenly feeling betrayed, realising that their trust was misplaced.

Guarding Our Heart

How do we guard our hearts from the poignant error of placing our trust in people who "look great" but eventually disappoint our expectations? We need to apply the principles of self-analysis revealed in the above architecture of deception, and subsequently apply them to others as well. Discovering what people value will reveal what decisions they will make in the future. Testing their character in small ways to discern levels of integrity is something that needs to be practised regularly. Be intentional about becoming more astute in observing and discerning if people are behaving in a deceitful manner.

From interviewing and testing potential candidates for intimate friendships to choosing a lifelong romantic partner – the stakes rise even higher. How can I divorce-proof my choice of marriage partner? Integrity, transparency, vulnerability and truthfulness are qualities that far surpass facial structure and body morphology. We need to train ourselves not to make superficial judgements; and to do this we must alter our own hidden set of values that we live by.

Many hearts are broken over shattered romantic hopes – where these hopes have been genuinely fuelled by charming smiles, friendly gestures, engaging conversations and allusions to a joyful future, but were ill-founded nevertheless. How can someone be charming, friendly and engaging; and at the same time, insincere and deceitful? People practise these behaviours knowingly or unknowingly in order to gain popularity, a temporary pleasure or a sense of security. Collateral damage is not on their radar. A trail of scarred hearts may follow behind their uncaring, unsympathetic, cavalier attitude to relationships.

Consequently the choice of a marriage partner needs to be scrutinised and assessed diligently by employing the sound principles as discussed in the charts in chapter 6. Clearly as Christians we need to pray and ask God for His constant guidance and witness of His Spirit as we work through this uncertain decision making domain. Learning to recognise the leading of God's Spirit is extremely important for our entire life – not just who to marry. (See Rick Godwin's *"Flying Higher"* for a fine outline of knowing God's will for our lives[89].)

Marital conflict can often arise not only because the other person's behaviour is interpreted to be offensive, but because our own hidden selfish agenda has been either exposed or denied satisfaction. "I want what

---

[89] Rick Godwin, *"Flying Higher. Seven keys to making Godly choices"* (1999) Creation House.

I want" and conflict ensues. Changing the "I want" to "How can I serve you?" often changes the context of a conflict situation.

Is it possible to avoid the pain and hurt of betrayal, broken trust and shattered expectations? If we want to be loving people, then there is an element of vulnerability when love reaches out and cares for others. If the person receiving the love responds selfishly it can hurt us since there was a hope that our love would be reciprocated.

Perhaps we can show love with no expectation or hope of any reciprocating relationship – but then there will be no relationship. Such a zero expectation leaves us walking away friendless even if a genuine friendship was offered in an authentic manner in return for the love shown.

To avoid the hurt of betrayal and rejection we have to close our heart to people, and to the possibility of a loving friendship or relationship. Even God gets hurt by those who reject Him:

Ezek 6:9 Then those of you who escape will remember Me among the nations where they are carried captive, because I was crushed by their adulterous heart which has departed from Me, and by their eyes which play the harlot after their idols; they will loathe themselves for the evils which they committed in all their abominations.

God does not harden His heart in order to avoid that pain, but continues to be vulnerable to the constant rejection of mere human beings by loving and caring for us. He is so great.

To pursue the immeasurable joy of lasting loving relationships, the vulnerability, transparency and risk of trusting people need to be embraced. Yes we will be disappointed and hurt at times, but a loving heart forgives and moves on to the next possibility of a great relationship based on integrity and agreed values.

Dr Henry Cloud gives us some lucid commentary on building trust delineating "Five essentials of Trust" in his recent book "Trust"[90]. These five essential elements to look for are: Understanding; Motive, Ability; Character and Track Record. If these essentials are observed, monitored and tested then building trust can be a much safer venture. Cloud goes on in his book to discuss an insightful seven step methodology for rebuilding trust with someone (example: an unfaithful spouse) who has broken trust. The last step includes "Eleven Indicators of Real Change" which provide a process for checking and holding the person accountable to prove actual change prior to being trusted again[91].

Ps 146: 3 Do not put your trust in princes, nor in a son of man, in whom there is no help.

SECTION B: HYPOCRISY – A PROFILE OF DECEPTION AND DECEITFULNESS

Hypocrites are people who say one thing, and yet do another. As Jesus outlined for us: *"but do not do according to their works; for they say, and do not do".* (Matt 23:3) This type of deceitfulness is rampant in our society. People can swear in public and make out to be corrupt in order to gain peer approval, but on their own, they do not do these things. Or the converse, where people pretend to be nice but later behave disreputably when with other people. This type of behaviour is common because of the beneficial short term gain amongst those they seek to influence. Nevertheless, the hypocritical heart will eventually be revealed for its dishonesty, deceit and lack of integrity.

Jesus was strong in His condemnation of the religious leaders who were hypocrites in His day.

---

[90] Dr Henry Cloud, *"Trust. Knowing when to give it, When to withhold it, How to earn it, and How to fix it when it gets broken"*, Worthy Publishing, (2023).
[91] Cloud, *ibid.*

Mark 7:6, 7 "Well did Isaiah prophesy of you hypocrites, as it is written: 'This people honours Me with their lips, but their heart is far from Me. And in vain they worship Me, teaching as doctrines the commandments of men.'"

Religious hypocrites teach man's commandments (*Matt 16:12*), and distort God's doctrines, hindering people from inheriting all that God has for them (*Matt 23:13 For you shut up the kingdom of heaven against men*). Let's have a closer look at the profile provided in scripture of these hypocrites, so that we can weed out any hypocrisy that might have found itself tolerated in our own hearts:

- Desire for man's approval – *But all their works they do to be seen by men.* (Matt 23:5); Matt 22:16 'You do not regard the face of man!' Jesus rejected man's approval. Man's approval is deceitful because it is centred on pleasing men more than God, so that there is no consistent set of values guiding the choice of words and actions. Their heart becomes like a chameleon – changing values to suit those currently present whose approval is desired. Man's approval is also divisive against those for whom it is excluded from. Man's approval implies "disapproval" for somebody else. This disapproval causes division and excludes people. Therefore man's approval is deceitful and divisive.
- Prey on people's weaknesses and want to appear good – *For you devour widows' houses, and for a pretense make long prayers.* (Matt 23:14);
- Do not live by example – *they themselves will not move them with one of their fingers* (Matt 23:4);
- Love for prominence – *They love the best places at feasts, the best seats in the synagogues* (Matt 23:5);
- Cannot discern true spiritual value – *Fools and blind! For which is greater, the gold or the temple that sanctifies the gold?* (Matt 23:17);
- Incorrect spiritual values – *For you pay tithe of mint and anise and cummin, and have neglected the weightier matters of the law: justice and mercy and faith.* (Matt 23:23);

- Only focus upon external appearance and do not value what is in the heart – *For you cleanse the outside of the cup and dish, but inside they are full of extortion and self-indulgence.* (Matt 23:25);
- Do not care about real holiness – *but inside are full of dead men's bones and all uncleanness.* (Matt 23:27);
- Lack in self-awareness – *we would not have been partakers with them in the blood of the prophets* (Matt 23:30);
- Hurt others without remorse – *some of them you will kill and crucify, and some of them you will scourge* (Matt 23:34);
- Cannot discern what is obvious – *but you cannot discern the signs of the times* (Matt 16:3);
- Pretentious and cunning – *But Jesus perceived their wickedness, and said, "Why do you test Me, you hypocrites?* (Matt 22:18).

HOW CAN WE OVERCOME DECEPTION?

Satan overcomes people easily if they embrace a deceiving line of thinking. History is replete with cases of erroneous thinking leading to failed ventures. Our journey towards success in life includes overcoming and avoiding the barrage of deceit launched at us by our spiritual enemy.

Hammond makes the insightful statement that *"Satan cannot defeat me in any area of my life unless he can first deceive me"*[92]. Unfortunately this is not entirely true, since we know that Adam was not deceived when he sinned and disobeyed God (1Tim 2:14) and yet Adam was defeated.

We can certainly invert this statement to read: *"If I am deceived in a particular area, then for this specific weakness I will be an easy target for the enemy to defeat me!"* We have discussed the severe consequences of deception in order to build determination in our hearts to resist and renounce every form of avenue of attack that might lead to deception in our lives.

---

[92] Mac Hammond, *"Doorways to Deception – How deception comes, how it destroys and how you can avoid it"*, Harrison House, Tulsa, Oklahoma (1999).

How do we overcome deception? Deception is a stronghold and it takes wisdom to dismantle it:

Prov 21:22 A wise man scales the city of the mighty and brings down the stronghold in which they trust.

We must expose every area by which we can possibly be deceived and reverse its influence and negate its lies. The next chapter attempts to do this. But the following 4 key principles are outlined as a high level strategy:

1. Pursuing The Truth

Truth is what corresponds to reality. Something is false if it does not correspond to reality. Deception encompasses lies shaded by the truth; or the truth coloured by lies. Each statement needs to be investigated and tested for its veracity before being received and believed.

1Thess 5:21 Test all things; hold fast what is good.

Correct doctrine and understanding of the truth is essential in overcoming misconceptions and deceptions, viz:

Job 42:7 And so it was, after the LORD had spoken these words to Job, that the LORD said to Eliphaz the Temanite, "My wrath is aroused against you and your two friends, for you have not spoken of Me what is right, as My servant Job has."

God wants us to speak correctly about Him, so that we do not misrepresent the Lord. Fundamentally, we can overcome satan's deception by pursuing spiritual truth which is found in the Word of God:

John 8:31, 32 "If you abide in My word, you are My disciples indeed. And you shall know the truth, and the truth shall make you free."

We also need to practise asking the question *"What is true in this situation?"* We see in John 18 that Pilate's heart was so hard that he had come to a point of disdaining even the concept of truth, that it was not relevant in his world of power, greed and control:

*John 18:37, 38 "For this cause I was born, and for this cause I have come into the world, that I should bear witness to the **truth**. Everyone who is of the **truth** hears My voice." Pilate said to Him,* **"What is truth?"**

Jesus summarises His life's mission by declaring that He was born to declare witness to the truth! As followers of Jesus Christ it is incumbent upon us to drive out any deception that the Holy Spirit highlights so we can walk in the truth as much as possible.

The Son of God instructs us that He who does the truth comes to the Light

John 3:19–21 "And this is the condemnation, that the light has come into the world, and men loved darkness rather than light, because their deeds were evil. For everyone practicing evil hates the light and does not come to the light, lest his deeds should be exposed. But he who does the truth comes to the light, that his deeds may be clearly seen, that they have been done in God."

If we practise doing what we know is wrong then we will keep ourselves in darkness. If we practise pursuing truth by doing what we know is right, then we will come to greater understanding of the spiritual realm and reality. Deception always leads away from truth into a greater unreality.

Psalm 51:6 Behold, You desire truth in the inward parts, and in the hidden part You will make me to know wisdom.

1Tim 2:4 God desires all men to be saved, and to come to the knowledge of the truth.

Those who decide to be deceitful lose interest in what is true. They do not want to know the truth. The apostle John writes about the importance of truth 5 times in the first 4 verses in his second epistle. He goes on to mention deceivers in verse 7. He mentions truth 7 times in 14 verses in his third epistle.

2 John 1, 2 The Elder, to the elect lady and her children, whom I love in truth, and not only I, but also all those who have known the truth, ² because of the truth which abides in us and will be with us forever, …

2. Receiving A Love For The Truth

Not only do we need to pursue the truth, but we need to love the truth. Why love the truth in an age of compromise, complacency and deceit? Because joy and peace and freedom come when we know the truth of the Word of God! Deception only increases if we do not love the truth.

*2Thess 2:9,10 The coming of the lawless one is according to the working of Satan, with all power, signs, and lying wonders, and with all unrighteous deception among those who perish, **because they did not receive the love of the truth**, that they might be saved.*

1Thess 2:13 when you received the word of God which you heard from us, you welcomed it not as the word of men, but as it is in truth, the word of God, which also effectively works in you who believe.

2Thess 2:13 because God from the beginning chose you for salvation through sanctification by the Spirit and belief in the truth.

3. Asking God to Show Us!

God wants us to regularly ask for wisdom (James 1:5) and similarly He desires us to continually ask Him for direction regarding guidance and decision making in order to avoid deception. In matters where we already have a level of deception we need to ask God to reveal that to us:

Ps 139:23, 24 Search me, O God, and know my heart; try me, and know my anxieties; ²⁴ And see if there is any wicked way in me, and lead me in the way everlasting.

Phil 3:15 Therefore let us, as many as are mature, have this mind; and if in anything you think otherwise, *God will reveal even this to you.*

Psalm 19:12, 14 Who can understand his errors? Cleanse me from secret faults. … [14] Let the words of my mouth and the meditation of my heart be acceptable in Your sight, O Lord, my strength and my Redeemer.

This is particularly important for a church leader who rashly promotes someone who appears very friendly (like an "angel"), places trust in them, and is later devastated and discouraged by the betrayal and departure of that person.

4. Aligning our values to those of the Kingdom of God!

As discussed above, satan's children align their values with those of their father satan. Similarly God wants His children to fully align our values with His! Jesus was completely aligned to His Father such that the enemy had nothing in Him. In order to protect ourselves from deception we need to align our own values to those of the Kingdom of God. To do this without hypocrisy we need to ask the Holy Spirit to continually realign us when our actions are out of alignment with His will.

CONCLUSION

The good news is that we can overcome all forms of deception! If we follow the Lord and trust in Him with all of our heart, then we can be confident that the God of truth and veracity will lead us into all truth, liberty and freedom, and out of any deception that may be harboring in our hearts. This is a great comfort to those of us who have been tricked by the devil's cunning in the past and have made unwise choices – we can get better at detecting satan's wiles and devices. Thank God! Of course it means that we need to let go of some things we might treasure – such as popularity and man's approval. The fear of rejection can be a strong motivator, but we need to hide our heart in the Spirit.

Chapter Review

In this chapter we looked at basic lies that cause confusion and deception, and why people practice deceit. A detailed profile of hypocrisy was provided and 4 ways to overcome deception were discussed:

Pursuing The Truth; Receiving A Love For The Truth; Asking God to Show Us; and Aligning our values to those of the Kingdom of God (*key words:* pursuing, receiving, asking, aligning).

How Do We Respond?

Man's approval and hypocrisy are almost ubiquitous. How often do we value what people think of us — without considering what God thinks of us?

I suspect we suffer from some of its tentacles at least at some juncture in our lives. When was the last time we detected man's approval operating through our words?

Have we been hypocritical in our thoughts? Preaching purity but lusting after women in our hearts?

This insidious enemy needs to be weeded out from our lives, because it results in elitism and division amongst God's people.

Let us be diligent to recognize, discern its operation, and remove it both from our own hearts and from the unspoken values in our church.

John 5: 41, 44 "I do not receive honour from men" ...[44] "How can you believe, who receive honor from one another, and do not seek the honor that comes from the only God?"

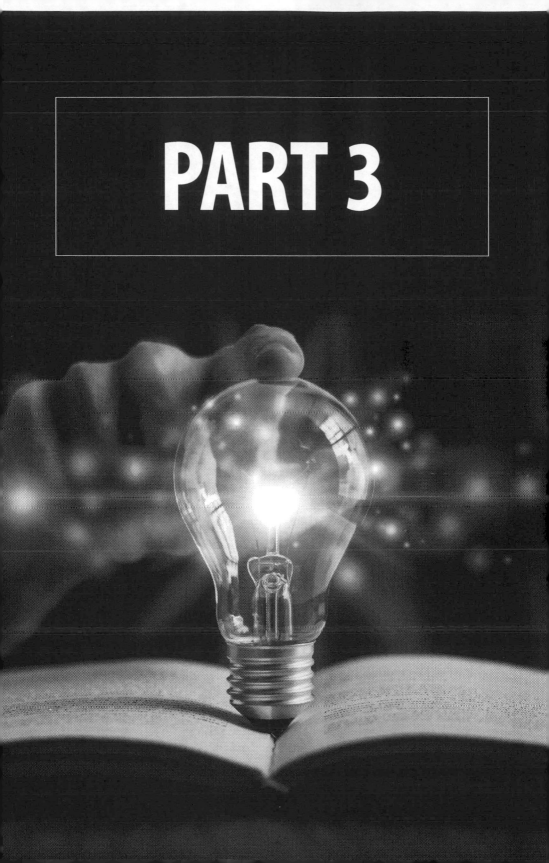

PART 3

APPLICATION OF THE ARCHITECTURES OF WISDOM AND TRUTH

Prov 24:3,4 Through wisdom a house is built, and by understanding it is established; by knowledge the rooms are filled with all precious and pleasant riches.

I f we apply the architecture of wisdom to our heart with a sincere desire to learn, grow and practise its spiritual principles then we will grow in wisdom. We can avoid deception in our lives if we try to minimise everything that is outlined in the architecture of deception, and apply the architecture of truth (see Chart 3 below). By doing these things we can increase in wisdom, peace and clarity of thought.

Houses are complex and require an architectural blueprint

The design of a house determines how we build it. What design do we have for creating our spiritual house? We live in and with the fruit of our own words and actions. A foolish woman tears down or destroys her own house:

Prov 14: 1 The wise woman builds her house, but the foolish pulls it down with her hands.

An architecture is the design, blueprint or the list of instructions on how to construct and build a designated structure.

The Man who Cut Corners: During one of his podcasts, Joel Osteen told a story of a man contracted to build a house with a $200,000 budget. The owner left everything into the trust of the builder. The builder cut corners on the budget and managed to trim $40,000 off the budget so that he could keep that cash for himself and still satisfy the owner with a house that appeared externally to be equivalent to that requested. The builder used cheaper material, watered down the concrete, thinner wooden boards, thicker layers of mortar and less brick, thinner wiring, then covered the shortcuts with gyprock and paint. When the owner came to look over the house, he was impressed because it did look good. He then turned to the builder and said, "Look, here are the keys to the house, it is actually a gift to you – I have wanted to bless you for some time!" The builder could not believe it. If he had known he was building his own house he would not have cut corners!

The moral of this story to have integrity and faithfulness in business and in life is clear. The extension I would like to make to this moral is that we are all building our own house, we only have one house, and we live in that house! Are we going to take pleasure seeking, compromising shortcuts, or will we take the hard road and make quality decisions that will last us for the long haul? The house that we live in becomes a testament to the decisions we have made thus far in our lives.

We are all building our own house – what type of house are we building?

Every building has an architecture from which it is built

Many cities have a preceding architecture governing their construction and design. Each motor car we see on the road had a descriptive architecture to guide its construction (sometimes with numerous layers). Anything that has been built to last has almost always had an architecture to guide and delimit its assembly or construction.

We could therefore infer that God created the universe from an architectural description of what He wanted to build. The universe is so complex and extremely finely tuned for the existence of biological life that it would be inconceivable that God did not have an architecture in mind for the entire universe before He created it.

My guess is that the Godhead initially would have counseled together and decided what type of life forms were to be designed with what DNA code for existence on earth: those which were to be completely instinct based, soul based, or those with a spirit base to their formation. This design (architecture) would have included the commensurate level of IQ (intellectual capacity, if any) of all of the animals, birds and plants.

Once the type of carbon based life forms were decided upon – their detailed metabolic sequences had to be outlined before even the universe was made. Why? Because the material required for our bodies to function could only be manufactured from a 3rd stage supernova that had formed heavy trace elements in its explosive activity right from the foundation of the earth.

God needed to create an earth-like planet in which Cu, Fe and Zn and other heavy elements existed so that He could construct the first life forms. Without these elements He could not create life from "the dust of the earth". Consequently God's architectural design included all of the biological necessities required for life before the universe began! God is incredibly detailed and awesome.

An Architecture for Our House

The house we build has an architecture guiding its construction. (See Chart 1 below). This architecture consists of the differing components of what we value and moral principles that we build into the foundation of our relationships.

If our house consists of the set of important relationships in our lives – then our architecture governs how those relationships will grow and develop. This architecture can have in it anything we value.

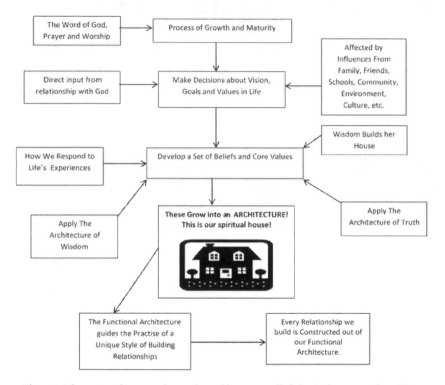

Chart 1: The spiritual state we live in has a blueprint called the Architecture of our House

Matt 7: 24, 25 "Therefore whoever hears these sayings of Mine, and does them, I will liken him to a wise man who built his house on the rock: [25] and the rain descended, the floods came, and the winds blew and beat on that house; and it did not fall, for it was founded on the rock.

What is our spiritual house like?

Our house consists of the consequences of every human relationship we have ever had – and how we have practiced responding to them: whether with love, acceptance and forgiveness; or with rejection, hatred or bitterness, for example.

If we value getting our own way above how we treat others, then abuse, manipulation, domination and control will be seen to be expedient to achieve our goals – then these will be in our architecture and will govern and affect our personal relationships. If we value love, joy, patience and integrity then these will feature in our architecture, and our relationships will begin to reflect what we value.

CONCLUSION: BUILDING OUR SPIRITUAL HOUSE DAY BY DAY

Let us define a precious stone as having a perfumed fragrance and emitting a bright coloured light. Prov 24:3,4 tells us that our "rooms are filled with all precious and pleasant riches". Let us define a black rock as having a pungent stench to it and that which absorbs light – so it produces darkness.

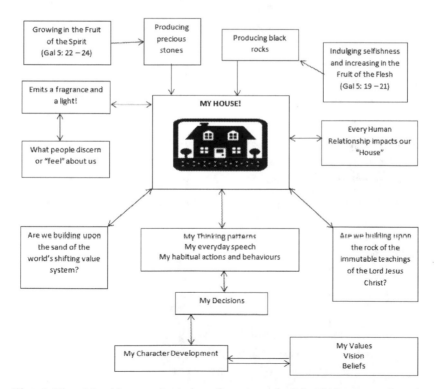

Chart 2: The spiritual house we live in has a fragrance and a light which emanates from the precious stones and black rocks that we have stored and accumulated. (Luke 11:34–36).

The number of precious stones or black rocks we have in our house depends upon our decisions. These thoughts are outlined diagrammatically in Chart 2 above. A precious stone might be how we have behaved with love, joy, peace, integrity, holiness, faith, righteousness, forgiveness, obedience or God-centredness.

A black rock might be the result of thinking about or behaving with jealousy, anger, shouting, adultery, conflict, drunkenness, betrayal, treachery, self-centeredness, bitterness or hatred (or other carnal behavior, as listed in Gal 5:19–21). The Lord Jesus elaborates these principles when He stated:

Luke 11:34–36 The lamp of the body is the eye. Therefore, when your eye is good, your whole body also is full of light. But when your eye is bad, your body also is full of darkness. [35] *Therefore take heed that the light which is in you is not darkness.* [36] **If then your whole body is full of light, having no part dark, the whole body will be full of light,** *as when the bright shining of a lamp gives you light."*

Chapter Review

The spiritual house we live in has a fragrance and a light which emanates from precious stones and black rocks that we have stored and accumulated in our house (Chart 2). Below in chart 3 is an outline of the components required in pursuing the truth and overcoming the pitfalls of deception.

How Do We Respond?

Prov 9:1 Wisdom has built her house; she has hewn her seven pillars.

The house that wisdom builds has seven pillars – are we strengthening these pillars in our lives or weakening them with our decisions each day?

Each house will emit a fragrance and a light – affected by the number of black rocks or precious stones present – how does our house shine and how does it smell?

What affect are we having upon people around us?

How much love do we have in our close personal relationships?

How much joy and peace is in our marriage?

Take time to look through the Architecture of Truth (Chart 3). Which aspect of this description is lacking in our own lives?

Can we write down areas that need attention and hold ourselves accountable to develop those areas?

Remember the architecture of deception – be careful to weed out all of these insidious forces that will lead us astray.

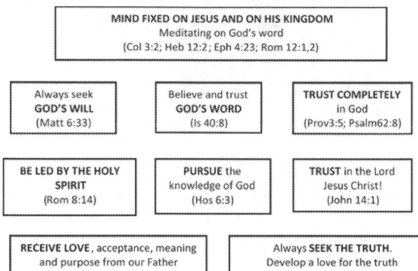

MIND FIXED ON JESUS AND ON HIS KINGDOM
Meditating on God's word
(Col 3:2; Heb 12:2; Eph 4:23; Rom 12:1,2)

Always seek **GOD'S WILL** (Matt 6:33)	Believe and trust **GOD'S WORD** (Is 40:8)	**TRUST COMPLETELY** in God (Prov3:5; Psalm62:8)
BE LED BY THE HOLY SPIRIT (Rom 8:14)	**PURSUE** the knowledge of God (Hos 6:3)	**TRUST** in the Lord Jesus Christ! (John 14:1)

RECEIVE LOVE, acceptance, meaning and purpose from our Father (Rom 5:5, 8)

Always **SEEK THE TRUTH**. Develop a love for the truth (John 3:21; 2Thess 2:10).

COURAGE and Security (Josh 1:5, 9)

SINCERE LOVE and care for others (John 13:35)

HOLINESS and Purity (Lev 11:44)

IMPARTIAL and God's approval (James 2:9; John 5:41)

Humility   Honesty   Love for Truth   Integrity
(1Pet 5:5;   Eph 4:25;   Eph 4:15;   Psalm 26:1)

Obedience   Righteous   Lawful
(1Sam 15:22   Rom 3:21,22   1Tim 1:8,9)

SUBMISION   FAITH   GOD'S WILL
(James 4:6;   Mark 11:22;   John 5:30; 8:29)

Chart 3: A Spiritual Architecture For Truth: To be applied with prayer, meditation and obedience. An outline of the components required in pursuing the truth and overcoming the pitfalls of deception (this is the inverse of the architecture of deception).

CONCLUSION AND WISDOM CHART

1Cor 3:9,10 For we are God's fellow workers; you are God's field, you are God's building. [10] According to the grace of God which was given to me, as a wise master builder I have laid the foundation, and another builds on it. But let each one take heed how he builds on it.

The kingdom of God needs many "wise master builders" who can lay foundations for churches and set systems in place that will see the church flourish with much growth and joy. As church leaders and pastors grow in wisdom they can see a generation of young people trained to rise up with a wisdom beyond their years and ahead of their tutors.

In the coming years being a Christian influence and witness in the 21st century will become more complex, nuanced and even dangerous. The wisdom of God will be paramount in tense circumstances, but Jesus promised us irrefutable wisdom if only we practise walking with Him and listening to His Spirit.

Common flaws of self-centredness and self-promotion will need to be obviated and our lives "hidden with Christ in God". This will enable us to be the pure vessels that the Lord seeks to use in these desperate times when eternal life is in the balance.

Everyday people are making decisions about God and whether they should place their faith in the Lord Jesus Christ.

Let us do our best for the Lord and for His people, amen.

Prov 24:3,4 Through wisdom a house is built, and by understanding it is established; by knowledge the rooms are filled with all precious and pleasant riches.

WISDOM SUMMARY CHART

We need to ask God for wisdom each day

Learn not to rely upon our own cognitive capacity but to seek wise counsel for our decisions

Pray for clarity and peace regarding all decision making

Remember trust is earned "You know his proven character"

Always try your best to get both sides of the story

We cannot tell if someone is lying to us

Deception is widespread and common – beware of charm and man's approval

Sincerely love, desire and seek the truth – especially about ourselves

Ask God to reveal to us any hidden motives which will help us to avoid self-deception

Be determined to build a quality, wise house for Jesus that will stand the tests

APPENDICES

THE SEVEN PILLARS
OF WISDOM

Discussed in more detail

UNDERSTANDING: is important in relating to others in that we need to appraise their situation accurately. This encompasses their upbringing, inherent weaknesses, current responsibilities, levels of stress, fear and insecurity – all contribute towards their actions and words. God understands and comprehends us, which is too "wonderful" for us (Psalm 139:1,2,6), so likewise it is incumbent upon us to strive to understand those whom we influence with our decisions, so as not to be harsh towards people (*Prov 10: 13 Wisdom is found on the lips of him who has understanding*).

This category can include empathy, where there is a deep connection with the pain and struggles of others (John 11:35). Consequently in making wise decisions, pursuing a better understanding of both sides of the situation and the factors involved is essential. Understanding one another's weaknesses also augments our ability to forgive transgressions – a man of understanding holds his peace (Prov 11:12). God is our source and we can always ask Him for more understanding, as God said to King Solomon, "See I have given you a wise and understanding heart" (1King 3:12).

A lack of understanding can persist in those who have a dismissive attitude (*"You'll get over it"*) based on contrary values (*"I don't care"*). A misunderstanding can occur for many reasons ranging from: miscommunication (*"I did not say that"*), misinterpretation (*"That is not what I meant"*), missing details (*"What?"*), being insensitive (*"You are insane"*) to simply being suspicious and not wanting to understand (*"What do you really mean?"*). All of these mistakes and bad attitudes need to be rectified if a good understanding can be attained of either the person or the situation.

KNOWLEDGE: If we are seeking to make a wise decision in any technical field, such as law, medicine, physics, epidemiology, childcare, then the development of knowledge in that area is mandatory. Knowledge is prerequisite in many areas of decision making (Prov 14:18b *The prudent are crowned with knowledge*). We should not overlook this, and simply assume we can make a wise decision without detailed study. For example, if a judge is to make a "wise judgement" then he must know recent changes to the state laws and their subtleties. Prov 24:5 *"A wise man is strong, yes a man of knowledge increases strength"*.

The enemy of knowledge is not so much ignorance but presumption and indolence. These foolish influences we need to guard against, especially if we become proud from previous achievements (1Cor 8:1) and are persuaded we can make decisions without due diligence. Today, knowledge is accessible at our finger tips and we should not allow a lack of knowledge to hinder our decision making.

EQUITY: is where everyone is treated fairly and equally, with the application of a system of justice that facilitates impartial judgement. In God's kingdom we see *"there is neither Jew nor Greek, there is neither slave nor free, there is neither male nor female; for you are all one in Christ Jesus"* (Gal 3:28) which conflates with the principal of not showing partiality – which is very important to God (James 2:1, 9; Gal 2:6, Rom 2:11). Therefore in our decision making we cannot allow man's approval or partiality to influence us – each human being must be treated equally based upon merit and character, not upon superficial qualities (such as gender, race, skin colour, financial status, intellectual status, career, talent, looks).

Isaiah 11:4 *"But with righteousness He shall judge the poor, and decide with equity for the meek of the earth"*. Operating with equity then is a wonderful attribute of wisdom where judgement is impartial and external observers can vindicate the decision made. Conversely, man's approval is a subtle spirit that appeals to the eye (*"I'm looking good"*) to the taste (*"I am a success!"*) and to one's desire to be popular (*" finally I'm secure"*). Insecurity causes us to stumble over this temptation to receive the approval and praise from others (rather than from the Lord). The trap is that man's approval is divisive – because it divides against those who are the "unapproved", and exacerbates insecurity rather than cures it. Thus we will earn God's disapproval for showing partiality due to someone's charm toward us (James 2:9).

Therefore another enemy of wisdom is man's approval and pride – whose fruit we can train ourselves to recognise and remove from our hearts.

DISCRETION: provides a scope of choice in decision making within guidelines (Prov 5:1,2 that you may preserve discretion), for example a cultured woman being given the freedom to choose her own dress for the president's ball. In the Australian military there is "discretionary command" where a platoon or section leader is given an objective to achieve ("Take that hill") but with some discretion as to how to complete the mission ("Attack from the left at night"). A commander should not give highly detailed orders to be carried out, due to the "fog of war" and dynamic changes in the battlespace.

Likewise in our course of action to achieve our vision and mission for the Lord Jesus Christ our enemy will throw unanticipated curve balls that can dislodge our momentum for a time. This is where discretionary changes in approach or strategy are essential in order to circumvent problems or to overcome setbacks. In a church structure empowering the leaders means to delegate authority to those closest to the situation to make the best decision. This aspect of wisdom is crucial in a real war, but it is more important in the spiritual warfare that we are constantly engaged in for the spirits and souls of many people. *Prov 11:30 "The fruit of the righteous is a tree of life, and he who wins souls is wise."*

Our enemy in this case is the age old form of witchcraft that creeps into the church through a desire for control. Rather than provide for discretionary decision making, the leader prescribes orders in detail with no scope of variation. This can eventually lead to unwise decisions being made and result in a frustrated team.

DISCERNMENT: is the ability to discern between right and wrong, good and evil, and to judge people or things accurately. The discerning of spirits (mentioned in 1Cor 12:10) is a great attribute in choosing between two or more candidates for a marriage, a business proposition, or a leadership position, where discerning the motive of the heart is crucial for a long term relationship. Building a team of leaders requires a culture of loyalty, unity, humility, submissiveness and obedience yet with strength, initiative and drive. These qualities can take some time to discriminate from a background of impressive words, charm and man's approval.

Prov 16:21 (ESV) The wise of heart is called discerning, and sweetness of speech increases persuasiveness.

Eccl 8:5b And a wise man's heart discerns both time and judgment …

For a church leader, discernment is not always an ethical choice (right or wrong) but can be the difference between a good idea and a better idea. When church growth is at stake, subtleties in decision making regarding apparently innocuous matters (colour of paint on the walls of the main hall, size of the entrance doorway, renovating the toilet or the kitchen first) can actually affect whether flighty visitors can relax and rest in a peaceful environment. If the "atmosphere" feels uneasy, rushed or stressed, visitors will move on unknowing as to why they felt uncomfortable – but church leaders need to know why they didn't stay. Hence discerning your people as a church leader is indispensable.

Heb 5:14 "But solid food belongs to those who are of full age, that is, those who by reason of use have their senses exercised to discern both good and evil."

The enemy of discernment is compromise that diminishes distinctions between right and wrong, good and better, and being spirit-led or not.

JUDGEMENT: is the ability to form valuable opinions and make good decisions; or to make an official legal decision. Eventually after weighing up the evidence concerning a matter we all have to make a decision, and this decision will have some level of "judgement" associated with it, where we are rejecting a foolish option and pursuing what we believe to be a wise option. A person of responsibility whose decisions affect the lives of others, will make judgements that are important and essential for the progress and development of all those concerned.

The apostle Paul encourages the church leader to maintain a high biblical standard of conduct in the church by recommending excommunication for the stubbornly unrepentant (1Cor 5:12,13) and to exercise wisdom in judgement in church matters (1Cor 6:2,3). Reluctance to make such decisions and ensuing judgements can leave the church in disarray, as a leader slow to set direction breeds confusion. As Craig Groeschel often remarks, *"the problem then becomes the leader themselves"*.

Of course our attitude in making judgements can be as important as the judgement itself. In Luke 6:37 Jesus warns us saying, "Judge not, and you shall not be judged. Condemn not, and you shall not be condemned." (similar to the exhortation in Matt 7:1). My understanding is that this is not precluding all judgement – as Jesus later advised "Do not judge according to appearance, but judge with righteous judgment." (John 7:24). Therefore the attitude of condemnation and self-aggrandisement is to be rejected in making necessary judgements.

The enemies of sound, wise judgement are the rejection of wise counsel, (e.g. by Rehoboam 1Kin 12:13) procrastination and confusion.

JUSTICE: without an agreed coherent set of ethical values that a society can live and abide by, the application of justice becomes weaker because the laws are changing relative to the shifting values of the populace in that era. In order for justice to provide a strong supporting structure to a society, that society must have a clear set of laws based on agreed values, with commensurate punitive measures for transgressors.

Peace, law and order prevail when "justice is done" and penalties are meted out to those to whom they are due without partiality. In setting up the foundation of a society or an organisation, such as in the wording of a constitution, wisdom, judgement and a keen appreciation of justice are required. Justice is therefore an important component of operating in wisdom, especially for a person in a senior position of authority (a King or Governor) who will need to make impartial assessments and unbiased applications of the laws of their organisation, province or country. One good example is that of Ezra who helped rebuild Jerusalem:

Ezra 7:25 And you, Ezra, according to your God-given *wisdom*, set magistrates and judges who may *judge all the people* who are in the region beyond the River, all such as know the laws of your God; and teach those who do not know them.

The enemies of justice are fear of man, a set of corrupt, selfish values and partiality to minority groups. In 1Sam 19 (and onwards) King Saul sought to kill David because of his own jealousy and insecurity (fear) which led him to make a whole series of unjust decisions. Likewise King David made unwise decisions due to his partiality regarding his own son Absalom (2Sam 18, 19).

THE ARCHITECTURE
OF DECEPTION

A description of each component

SIN: is clearly the main source of deception in our lives:

Heb 3:13 but exhort one another daily, while it is called "Today," lest any of you be hardened through the *deceitfulness* of sin.

James 1:15, 16 Then, when desire has conceived, it gives birth to sin; and sin, when it is full-grown, brings forth death. Do not be deceived, my beloved brethren.

Rom 7:11 For sin, taking occasion by the commandment, *deceived* me.

1 Cor 6:9 Do you not know that the unrighteous will not inherit the kingdom of God? Do not be *deceived*.

Not everyone is necessarily deceived if they sin. But the very nature of sin, is deceitful, therefore it is definitely a fine line to continue in sin and not be deceived about the consequences of sin:

1Tim 2:14 And Adam was not deceived, but the woman being deceived, fell into transgression.

The apostle Paul writes that "we ourselves were also once … deceived" when we served our own indulgences:

Titus 3:3 For we ourselves were also once foolish, disobedient, deceived, serving various lusts and pleasures, living in malice and envy …

If these false promises (lies) of sin are believed and embraced then the practise of sin leads into further levels of deception (Prov 14: 9,16).

PRIDE *(the quality of having an excessively high opinion of oneself or one's importance):*

Gal 6:3 For if anyone thinks himself to be something, when he is nothing, *he deceives himself.*

Obadiah 3, 4 The pride of your heart has *deceived* you, you who dwell in the clefts of the rock …

2 Tim 3:2, 7 For men will be lovers of themselves, lovers of money, *boasters, proud,* … [7] always learning and *never able to come to the knowledge of the truth.*

This phrase "never able to come to the knowledge of the truth" implies a deep level of deception that may never be exposed in the lives of those who are boastful and proud.

Isaiah spoke about the pride of the Babylonians "Your wisdom and your knowledge have warped *(led astray)* you; and you have said in your heart, 'I am, and there is no one else besides me.'" (Isaiah 47:10b). This is in line with the apostle Paul's comment that "knowledge puffs up *(or makes arrogant)* but love edifies" (1Cor 8:1b). For an unredeemed heart, the correlation between an unusual accumulation of knowledge and self-importance would normally lead the person astray with pride.

God not only resists us when we act in pride, but pride will itself deceive us. We must root out this sin, if we are to make wise decisions in our lives (Jer 48:29).

CHARM *(the power or quality of delighting, attracting, or fascinating others):*
Charm is portraying an image in order to sway another person for selfish interest or gain.

Prov 30:31 "Charm is *deceitful* and beauty is passing, but a woman who fears the Lord, she shall be praised."

Here we see clearly a person who practices being "charming" is being deceitful. Does this necessarily lead to them being deceived themselves? The principle is taken from 2 Tim 3:13 *(But evil men and impostors will grow worse and worse, deceiving and being deceived.)* where those who practice deception will themselves be deceived in some area of their lives.

Someone who practices telling lies, will most likely believe a lie themselves, and consequently be deceived. The obvious lie a liar believes is that "lying is profitable since I can get away with it".

Do not trust in those you don't know – who "write letters and bring presents" and flatter you. King Hezekiah was impressed with the importance of the envoys, letters and presents sent from the King of Babylon – and was most likely charmed by them (Is 39:2;2Chron 36:26,31).

HYPOCRISY *(acting or speaking in contradiction to stated beliefs or feelings):*

1Tim 4:1, 2 "some will depart from the faith, giving heed to *deceiving* spirits and *doctrines of demons*, speaking lies in *hypocrisy*, having their own conscience seared with a hot iron …"

Practising hypocritical behaviour leads directly to the deception of the person practising it. Hypocrisy is like a polite way to "lie". It cannot quite be pinned down (or exposed) easily, but those who practise it do not care about their own integrity –their priority is their personal agenda.

James discusses this lack of integrity (hypocrisy). He states that people who do not practise what they know is right, and display the appearance of a certain set of values will be deceived:

James 1:22 But be doers of the word, and not hearers only, *deceiving* yourselves.

James 1:26 If anyone … does not bridle his tongue but *deceives* his own heart …

Once I asked a hypocrite to explain to me what hypocrisy was. Interestingly they could not answer me coherently but mumbled some discombobulation.

LIES *(to make an untrue statement with intent to deceive):*

Prov 14:25 (ESV) A truthful witness saves lives, but one who breathes out lies is deceitful.

Prov 4:24 Put away from you a *deceitful* mouth, and put perverse lips far from you.

What we seek to prove is that a person who practises lying (with the intent to deceive others), will themselves be deceived. We cannot allow ourselves to pursue spiritual truth by relying upon our rational mind – as this can be misled. Many things might appear logical but that does not make them true. Therefore as usual – we need to be assiduous in our application of scripture if we want to prove a point. As with our intent in this whole book, we desire to reveal scripture that exposes sources of deception so that we can preclude their influence in our own personal lives.

The apostle Paul states that those who give heed to deceiving spirits are those who speak lies:

1Tim 4:1, 2 "some will depart from the faith, giving heed to *deceiving* spirits and *doctrines of demons*, speaking *lies* in hypocrisy, having their own conscience seared with a hot iron …"

If I give "heed to deceiving spirits" then by definition I will be led astray into deception. Therefore I believe it is possible to assert that those who practise lying will be deceived themselves (at least in some areas – including the discernment of right and wrong, as their consciences are seared).

Proverbs tells us that those who do evil will give heed to "false lips" and hence be deceived, and that those who lie will listen to other lies:

Prov 17:4 An evildoer gives heed to false lips; a liar listens eagerly to a spiteful tongue.

FEAR *(avoidance of doing something because one is afraid):* Fear of rejection, fear of failure or one of the innumerable different types of fear will lead us into worry and anxiety, and produce stress in our lives – causing us to stray from the peace, confidence and certainty that comes from walking by faith in God and trusting in Him.

Prov 29:25 The fear of man brings a snare, …

Isaiah warns that fear can lead to lies and subsequent deceitful behaviour:

Isaiah 57:11 "And of whom have you been afraid, or feared, that you have lied and not remembered Me, nor taken it to your heart?"

The apostle Paul reminds us that a spirit of bondage (possibly also deception) leads us into fear:

Rom 8:15 For you did not receive the spirit of bondage again to fear …

And the writer of Hebrews exhorts that the fear of death leads to a lifetime of bondage (and presumably some level of deception with it):

Heb 2:15 and release those who through fear of death were all their lifetime subject to bondage.

2 Tim 1:7 For God has not given us a spirit of fear, but of power and of love and of a sound mind.

Here Paul states that a sound mind (clarity in thought) can be achieved without fear. The inverse could be inferred to imply that a spirit of fear will lead us into an unsound (confused or deceived) mind.

SELFISH AMBITION *(to be self-seeking and looking out for one's own interests):* If we experience rejection early in our lives it is conceivable that we can become insecure. This insecurity can lead to unhealthy attitudes such as desiring attention, approval, or being first. Insecurity can link with comparison or competition (2Cor 10:12; Gal 6:4,5) giving rise to selfish ambition and jealousy. If these are not mitigated by the Holy Spirit then these attitudes can become a seed-bed for all sorts of wicked behaviour:

James 3:14 – 16 But if you have bitter envy and self-seeking in your hearts, do not boast and lie against the truth. This wisdom does not descend from above, but is earthly, sensual, demonic. For where envy and self-seeking exist, confusion and every evil thing are there.

"Every evil thing" would most likely include some level of deception, and "confusion" is indicative of some deception operating.

Gal 5:19 – 21 "the works of the flesh are evident … jealousies, … selfish ambitions, … that those who practice such things will not inherit the kingdom of God."

Those who practise selfish ambition are deceived into thinking that whatever self-gain they achieve is worthy of their effort.

Insecurity and selfish ambition are quite pervasive in our driven western societies such that even ministers can preach with wrong motives:

Phil 1:16 The former preach Christ from selfish ambition, not sincerely, supposing to add affliction to my chains;

Conversely the apostle Paul exhorts that nothing be done from selfish ambition!

Phil 2:3 Let nothing be done through selfish ambition or conceit, but in lowliness of mind let each esteem others better than himself.

SEDUCTION *(entice someone to do or believe something inadvisable or foolhardy):*

2Tim 3:13 But evil men and impostors will grow worse and worse, deceiving and being deceived.

The definition of the word seduction implies that some deception is operating when there is an attempt to seduce. While not a conclusion based upon God's word directly, the use of seduction by a person will usually fulfil the above verse, "*deceiving and being deceived*". Numerous verses link seduction to greater wickedness or more evil practises and thereby leading to calamity and judgement from God for those actions (Num 25:18; 2King 21:19; Prov 7:21; Ezek 13:10).

Secular research was conducted by Martin and Strudler, who studied seduction and deception and made the following conclusions:

"*Seduction almost always involves techniques of deception and self-deception, and risks trust and other moral goods we associate with truthfulness*"[93]. "Seduction, it will be plain, often involves deception. … A seducer can understand a person's weaknesses and wrongfully exploit those weaknesses without ever deceiving that person. *Much seduction, however, seems deceptive at its core.* The most successful seductions may involve both the exploitation of the weakness of the seduced and deception"[94].

Pornography and The Lust of the Flesh: Lust is deceiving because it promises fulfilment but leaves those who pursue it in an ever increasing grip for more. In his book, *"The Brain That Changes Itself"* Doidge[95] notes that pornography is as addictive as heroin and warps the neuron patterns in the human brain in the same manner as heroin warps the brain of an addict.

---

[93] Clancy Martin, Alan Strudler; *"Much Ado About Truth: On Seduction, Deception, and Self-deception"*, Humana Mente Journal of Philosophical Studies, (2012), Vol. 20, 246–264.

[94] Clancy Martin, *ibid.*

[95] Doidge, Norman, *"The Brain That Changes Itself" Stories of Personal Triumph from the Frontiers of Brain Science* (2007) Viking, Penguin Books Ltd.

2 Pet 2:14, 15 They are spots and blemishes, carousing in their own deceptions while they feast with you, having eyes full of adultery and that cannot cease from sin, enticing unstable souls.

Eph 4:21 – 23 put off … the old man which grows corrupt according to the deceitful lusts, and be renewed in the spirit of your mind.

PARTIALITY *(unfair bias in favour of one person or thing; favouritism, man's approval):* The authors of Deuteronomy and Chronicles both link showing partiality with taking bribes, where taking bribes blinds the eyes and twists the words:

Deut 16:19 You shall not pervert justice; you shall not show partiality, nor take a bribe, for a bribe blinds the eyes of the wise and twists the words of the righteous. (see 2 Chron 19:7).

Bribery is clearly linked to deception, but we cannot always link partiality with bribery.

James 2:4 "have you not shown partiality among yourselves, and become judges with evil thoughts?"

Is it possible to have evil thoughts without some level of deception? Probably not. As those who think evil in their heart obviously think that they can profit by employing such evil strategies. The apostle James links partiality with sin, so there must be some deception operating with those who practise partiality:

James 2:9b … but if you show partiality, you commit sin, and are convicted by the law as transgressors.

Jesus was able to teach the word of God in truth because He was not influenced by favouritism or the pressure to show partiality:

Luke 20:21b … You do not show personal favouritism, but teach the way of God in truth".

Favouritism: Is here implicitly linked with the inability to teach in truth – hence deception would be operating when people show favouritism and man's approval.

Man's Approval: Peter, thinking he knew best, took Jesus aside and reproved Him for thinking that God would allow Him to be crucified.

Jesus then rebuked Peter for being deceived by the devil; Peter had set his mind on man's interests (Matt 16:23).

Jesus exemplified victory over man's approval by rejecting the offer of honour from men: John 5:41 "I do not receive honour from men".

SATAN'S LIES: Jesus states that satan is the father of lies and that lying is part of his nature (John 8:44) – just as Jesus is the source of truth and cannot lie. He goes on to state that those who are satan's children cannot receive the truth or comprehend it. This implies that for satan's children there is a significant level of deception where truth is rejected in preference for lies (John 8:43, 46). Therefore the influence of satan's lies keeps them in deception and from knowing the truth. Satan deceives the nations and Jesus says he has "no truth in him" (John 8:44).

The serpent (the devil) is very crafty, and deceived Eve into eating of the forbidden fruit (also see 2Cor 11:3):

Gen 3:13 And the Lord God said to the woman, "What is this you have done?" The woman said, "The serpent deceived me, and I ate."

TRUST IN LIES:

Jer 7:4, 8 "Do not trust in these lying words, … ⁸ Behold, you trust in lying words that cannot profit."

Isaiah 28:15 For we have made lies our refuge, …

Hos 10:13 You have eaten the fruit of lies, because you trusted in your own way …

Isaiah 30:12 Because you despise this word, and trust in oppression and perversity, and rely on them ...

TRUST IN BEAUTY:

Ezek 16:15 "But you trusted in your own beauty, played the harlot because of your fame ..."

Ezekiel 28: 17 "Your heart was lifted up because of your beauty; you corrupted your wisdom for the sake of your splendor; I cast you to the ground, I laid you before kings, that they might gaze at you."

TRUST IN MAN: Unfortunately some of the most heart wrenching stories I have heard are those of betrayal by a "close friend". A man next to me on the plane to Dubai told me recently that his wife had betrayed him with his best friend only a few years ago. He was heartbroken at the time. It is an all too common scenario. Even brothers can lie to one another for selfish gain. The caveat for all of us is to be prudent, observant and slow to trust people.

Jer 17:5 Thus says the Lord: "Cursed is the man who trusts in man and makes flesh his strength, whose heart departs from the Lord" (also see Isaiah 30:2b,3).

The Lord Jesus did not put His trust in men (John 2:24, 25). And Jeremiah was warned by God regarding trusting in man when his society was wicked (Jer 9:4–6). Also see Micah 7:5.

TRUST IN RICHES: The gospel of Mark aligns the desire for riches and deceit:

Mark 4:19 "Now these are the ones sown among thorns; they are the ones who hear the word, and the cares of this world, *the deceitfulness of riches,* and the desires for other things entering in choke the word, and it becomes unfruitful."

Prov 11:28 He who trusts in his riches will fall, but the righteous will flourish like foliage.

Jer 48:7 For because you have trusted in your works and your treasures, you also shall be taken. And Chemosh shall go forth into captivity ...

The desire to be rich is a common snare and can lead into sin and deception – that money is more important than faith in God (Psalm 49:6, 7).

1Tim 6:8–10 But those who desire to be rich fall into temptation and a snare, and into many foolish and harmful lusts which drown men in destruction and perdition. For the love of money is a root of all kinds of evil ...

Do Not Trust in Our Own Heart: Trusting in our own heart and being led by our heart's desires will surely mislead us as the scripture warns against this:

Prov 28:26 He who trusts in his own heart is a fool, but whoever walks wisely will be delivered.

Jer 17:9 "The heart is deceitful above all things, and desperately wicked; who can know it?

REJECTING THE TRUTH (not loving the truth)

2 Thess 2:10–12 and with all unrighteous *deception* among those who perish, because they did not receive *the love of the truth*, that they might be saved. 11 And for this reason God will send them strong delusion, that they should *believe the lie*, 12 that they all may be condemned who did not believe the truth but had pleasure in unrighteousness.

Rom 1:21–25 ... became futile in their thoughts, and their foolish hearts were *darkened*. Professing to be wise, they became fools, ... who exchanged the truth of God for the *lie*

2 Tim 3:8 ... so do these also resist the truth: men of corrupt minds ...

2 Tim 4:4 ... and they will turn their ears away from the truth, and be turned aside to fables.

Rejecting the Knowledge of God and Right and Wrong: Some deny the knowledge of God and exchange the truth of God for a lie:

Rom 1:28 And even as they did not like to retain God in their knowledge, God gave them over to a debased mind, to do those things which are not fitting.

CONTRAST OF WISDOM WITH FOOLISHNESS
A list of comparisons

Prov 24: 7 Wisdom is too lofty for a fool; he does not open his mouth in the gate.

In Proverbs 9 both wisdom and foolishness cry out for the attention of mankind (Prov 9: 3,15). Due to the complex nature of wisdom and the difficulty in collating all its themes, I have attempted to contrast numerous characteristics of wisdom with is corresponding opposite. The more we expose the foolishness in our lives, the more we can learn to reject it. An article worth reviewing is by Banso who writes briefly about the sources and dangers of foolishness[96].

Henry Cloud advises: we can confront, rebuke, correct and give feedback to a wise man; but do not confront, rebuke, or correct a fool lest they hate

---

[96] Banso, Olanike O. *The Danger Of Foolishness* https://cedarministry.org/the-danger-of-foolishness/

you. He goes on to suggest: "Lead a fool with consequences and structure", that entail clear tasks, responsibilities and consequences[97].

Anger is not wise: Some justify anger by tacitly assuming "Anger is good, because when I get angry, I get what I want!" This is very bad thinking. A wise man keeps cool under pressure as Hezekiah did.

James 1: 19, 20 "let every man be swift to hear, slow to speak, slow to anger; [20] *for the anger of man does not produce the righteousness of God."* (Prov 14:17a A quick-tempered man acts foolishly.)

Our most precious relationships are in marriage and in our family, and if we allow our anger to go unchecked, we can hurt those we love. We can learn how to keep cool, calm, collected and composed. For example, we need to be careful not to judge one another for being different to us. If we are angry we might struggle to clearly describe what we are feeling; or we may analyse words logically and miss the emotional importance of what is being communicated.

CHARACTERISTICS OF THE WISE	CHARACTERISTICS OF THE FOOLISH
Pure motive and heart (James 3:17) – sexual immorality is unwise (1Cor 6:16).	*Impure* – crude, self-centred, pornographic, corrupt, earthly, sensual, demonic (James 3:15)
Peaceable (James 3:17) – calm, composed in the midst of the storm.	*Angry* – volatile, capricious, easily upset, violent countenance (James 1:20).
Gentle (James 3:17) – sensitive to others	*Rough* – pushy, insensitive, overly assertive
Willing to yield (James 3:17) – meekness usually matched with self-control.	*Unwilling* to yield 'I want my way', black is black, "I'm right, Your wrong!", dogmatic, intimidating
Full of mercy (James 3:17) – kind and forgiving of transgressions; (Prov 10:21).	*Fault-finding* – not mindful of people's background, experiences, hardships or weaknesses
Full of good fruits (James 3:17) abounds in love, joy, peace, goodness, kindness, self-control!	*Unrestrained:* Lacks self–control, not faithful, proud, unkind, stingy, hateful, unforgiving, selfish
Without partiality (James 3:17; Rom 2:11) and looks for the fruit of good character	*Favoritism* based on position / money / pedigree / dress / race / ability / intelligence
Without hypocrisy (James 3:17; Rom 12:9) not deceitful, having integrity of character	*Hypocritical* twists words and does not hold to integrity, changes values to suit the situation

---

[97] Henry Cloud, *The Evil, The Foolish, The Wise*, (2015) The Global Leadership Podcast; https://globalleadership.org/videos/leading-others/the-evil-the-foolish-the-wise

Faith in God and Jesus Christ *Ps 19:1*
The heavens declare the glory of God!

Does not believe in God or Jesus Christ *Ps 14:1*
The fool has said in his heart there is no God.

Fear of the Lord combined with an understanding of justice, right and wrong.

Does not fear or respect God *Rom 1:22*
Professing to be wise they became fools

Cries out and asks for more wisdom (James 1:5, Prov 1:20–22), recognizes a daily dependency upon the Lord

Does not ask God for help, nor seeks for wisdom; proud and self-confident. (Zech 7:13; Prov 1:28-30).

Builds on the Rock and is determined to apply Jesus' teachings to life (Matt 7:25)

Builds on the sand, of contemporary thinking or of friends opinions and feelings.

Judges situations carefully, and recognizes that lives may be at stake (1King 3:16–28)

Makes rash judgements without thinking *Hos 7:11 Ephraim also is like a silly dove, without sense*

Wise Counsel: Makes decisions based on wise counsel of those spiritually mature (Prov 15:22)

Makes his own decisions, self-seeking (James 3:14; Rom 2:8). No time to seek for wisdom.

Allows for men and women to behave, think and react differently, and makes allowances (1Pet 3:7).

Judges harshly, without being considerate or sensitive or trying to understand their different feelings

Makes friends easily – a wise man saves souls (Prov 11:30) and is popular (David 1Sam 18:5, 30)

Lonely: preoccupied with self and isolates himself (Prov 18:1) does not really care about others.

Content with what we have (*1Tim 6:8 having food and clothing, with these we shall be content.*) unafraid of rivals – not competitive (Gal 6:4,5).

Bitter envy and jealousy, 2Cor 10:12 But they measuring themselves by themselves … are not wise. (James 3:14) comparing with others (Gal 6:4,5).

Merciful: Not judging one another (*James 2:13 Mercy triumphs over judgment*). Rom 14:4 Who are you to judge another's servant? To his own master he stands or falls. Indeed, he will be made to stand, for God is able to make him stand. Col 2:16

Judgmental and fault finding, James 2:13 "Judgement is without mercy to one who has shown no mercy" – judges the weak, young, poor, untalented etc. (Rom 2:1, 3; James 4:11, 12 Do not speak evil of one another.)

Accepts people as they are (Eph 1:6) and celebrates their differences (unity in diversity).

Rejects people who differ to themselves – shows partiality, and pride of life.

Leadership Qualities of wisdom and understanding are required for the position of leadership (Deut 1:13, Prov 8:15, 16)

Fools despise wisdom, instruction (Prov 1:7) and knowledge, and love simplicity (Prov 1:22); where a foolish leader causes people to groan.

Saves a city from military conflict (2Sam 20:16 –22) a wise woman cried out from the city "Hear!"

A fool's mouth calls for blows – a fool will often stir up strife (Prov 18:6).

Understands the times: Esth 1:13 "*Then the king said to the wise men who understood the times*" 1Chron 12:32 '*who had understanding of the times*'. God may provide an "open door" (1Cor16:9) for a season to be recognized and capitalized upon.

A fool is ignorant of impending danger (Lot's sons-in-law in Gen 19:14) or the significance of certain timing (Esth 4:14), or the fact that people close or open their hearts over a specific window of time and opportunity (Jonah and Nahum).

Young people can be wiser than the aged, the young are not always foolish (Job 32:7, 8)

The old are not always wise, Nor do the aged always understand justice (Job 32:9).

Uses time carefully *Teach us to number our days* that we may gain a heart of wisdom (Ps 90:12) Walk in wisdom toward those who are outside, *redeeming the time* Col 4:5

Wastes Time Allows their days to pass by. Eph 5:15, 16 "See then that you walk circumspectly, not as fools but as wise, *redeeming the time, because the days are evil*"

Meditates on the word of God Ps 119:99 I have more understanding than all my teachers, for Your testimonies are my meditation.

Oblivious of God and His ways, have a shallow philosophy of life, self-centred, focused on pleasure or their own success (2 Tim 3:2 – 4).

Observant +understanding: Ps 107:43 Whoever is wise will observe these things and they will understand the lovingkindness of the Lord; Prov 8:33 Hear instruction, be wise, do not disdain it.

Fools are not observant of the way God deals with men or nations. They can rush in without thinking, or taking time to observe behaviors or various events and actions.

Seeks God's will: Eph 5:17 do not be unwise but understand what the will of the Lord is.

A fool will not seek God's will, thereby fails to achieve their destiny and may not enter heaven.

A wise person accepts rebuke: Prov 9:8 – 9 "Rebuke a wise man, and he will love you. Give instruction to a wise man, and he will be still wiser; teach a just man, and he will increase in learning".

A fool does not accept rebuke Prov 9:7, 8 "He who corrects a scoffer gets shame for himself, and he who rebukes a wicked man only harms himself. Do not correct a scoffer, lest he hate you;"

Listens and Hears: A wise person will increase in learning (Prov 1:5; Prov 8:34)

A fool thinks he knows it all, and is slow to ask elders for advice or wise counsel.

Trusts in the Lord with all his heart: Prov 3:5,6 a wise person leans not on his own understanding, acknowledges the Lord in all of his ways – their paths will be made straight!

The fool is wise in his own eyes Prov 3:7 and does not trust in the Lord, does not acknowledge the sovereignty of God in day to day circumstances – their paths are rarely straight.

A wise man is happy (Prov 3:13; 8:35) – learning the secret of contentment in all things Phil 4:12 (And having food and clothing, with these we shall be content. 1Tim 6:8).

A fool is never satisfied. Prov 30:15 A leech has two daughters "*Give, Give*" (1Tim 6:9 those who desire to be rich fall into temptation and a snare, and into many foolish and harmful lusts …)

Peace: Wisdom brings pleasantness, peace, and a tree of life (Prov 3:17, 18)

A fool stirs up anger and contention *Prov 15:1,18 a harsh word stirs up anger, a wrathful man stirs up strife.*

Walks safely, with feet that will not stumble, or be afraid (Prov 3: 23, 24)

Stumbles into sin not realising its devastation Prov19:3 the foolishness of man twists his way

The wise shall inherit glory (*Prov 3:35a The wise shall inherit glory,*)

Shame shall be the legacy of fools (*Prov 3:35b But shame shall be the legacy of fools.*)

Strength **understanding and counsel** *Prov 8:14 Counsel is mine, and sound wisdom; I am understanding, I have strength.*

Weakness and poor health can come upon those who are not careful (*1Cor11:30 For this reason many are weak and sick among you*)

Turns away from immorality (Prov 7:5) A wise man shows sense and purity of heart.

Enjoys being flattered and is vulnerable to seduction (Prov 5:3 and Prov 7:5).

Self-Control: And everyone who competes for the prize is temperate in all things. (1Cor 9:25)

A fool is indulgent does not care about restraint 1Cor15:32 Let us eat and drink for tomorrow we die

Diligent and works hard (Prov 6:8, 11; Prov 10:5) Wisdom sees the importance of working hard.

The fool is lazy (Prov 6:6,9; Prov 10:5) is not concerned about the future, only enjoying oneself now.

Turns to God when Tempted: 1Cor 10:13 God is faithful, who will not allow you to be tempted beyond what you are able, but with the temptation will also make the way of escape (asking God for help), that you may be able to bear it.

Tries to overcome the fleshly temptations in their own strength. The bible clearly tells us that we overcome the flesh by the Spirit (Rom 8:13 and Gal 5:16) and that we should pray so as not to enter temptation (Mark 14:38).

Spiritually Discerning: 1Cor 2:13 These things we also speak, not in words which man's wisdom teaches but which the Holy Spirit teaches, comparing spiritual things with spiritual.

The natural man does not receive the things of the Spirit of God, for they are foolishness to him; nor can he know them, because they are spiritually discerned. (1Cor 2:14)

Wisdom does not isolate itself in time of distress or need, but turns to wise counsel (Prov 18:1 and Prov 11:14).

He who isolates himself seeks his own desire; He rages against all wise judgment (Prov 18:1) e.g. Lot chose for himself (Gen 13:11)

Focused, determined to succeed in the mission given from heaven (Acts 26:19).

Easily Distracted looking for amusement, not having a clear set of goals to live by

Clear Vision (Prov 29:18) and develops discipline and self-control by obeying the law.

Wanders Aimlessly (Prov 29:18) does not obey the law and does not practice self-control.

THE LIMITS OF MAN'S WISDOM

1Cor 2:4 And my speech and my preaching were not with persuasive words of human wisdom, but in demonstration of the Spirit and of power, that your faith should not be in the wisdom of men but in the power of God.

Wisdom will lead us to more success and greater strength, and wisdom is prerequisite for those in leadership and authority over and under others (*Prov 10: 8 The wise in heart will receive commands*). But wisdom is not a panacea. The balance in the New Testament is to have faith in the Spirit of God for regular guidance, wisdom and counsel – and also to have faith that God can do miracles where strategic options are no longer viable. Healing the sick, opening doors that are shut, God's power in ministry are now all part of the greater scope of and purview of wisdom.

Weaknesses of relying solely upon wisdom:

Wisdom is not a panacea;

Wisdom is not necessarily loving;

Not all problems can be solved with wisdom – some problems are caused by people who harden their hearts and refuse to do the right thing;

Wisdom is not necessarily passionate or zealous;

Wisdom in the past does not preclude us from future foolish decisions (e.g. Solomon, Hezekiah);

Familiarity with wisdom can lead to a reliance upon self.

Under the new covenant the "getting of wisdom" is no longer the principle thing – but being led by the Spirit is more important.

Being led by the Spirit is the goal; not only being wise – when we seek to be led by the Spirit we learn to depend upon the Lord each day for guidance;

Spirit led decision making surpasses wise decision making (where "wise" here can seem to be the most logical and reasonable option);

Wisdom does not deliver from iniquity – Lucifer was "full of wisdom" (Ezek 28:12) yet he sinned and rebelled against the Lord.

CONCLUSION

God commands us to be wise. We need to expose our own foolish behaviour, remove it from our lives and overcome it diligently. We can redeem our time: wisdom makes the most of every opportunity. We can decide today to grow in wisdom! To work hard, to commit to God's purposes in His church, and to be prudent and circumspect as to how we live. Meditating on God's word and reading the whole bible is hard work – but wisdom is its own reward.

EXPOSING OTHER WAYS WE CAN BE DECEIVED

2Cor 4:3,4 But even if our gospel is veiled, it is veiled to those who are perishing, 4 whose minds the god of this age has blinded, who do not believe, lest the light of the gospel of the glory of Christ, who is the image of God, should shine on them.

Tragically here we see why many of those who do not believe struggle to understand spiritual reality and principles of God's kingdom because their minds have been blinded by satan. For our mind to be "blind" it must mean that we cannot grasp, comprehend or "see" simple concepts and ideas that would lead us to faith in God. The blindness then must be a deception that people unknowingly live with.

The battlefield is the mind. The victory is believing and walking in the truth – taking every thought captive to the obedience of Christ each day (2Cor 10:5). The defeat is acquiescing to the lies and thereby embracing various levels of deception. If we:

claim to have no sin 1John 1:8 hear the word of God, but do not act on it James 1:22
practice fleshly indulgence Gal 6:7, 8
are unaccountable in speech James 1:26

are bitter and unforgiving 1John 2:11

listen to crafty arguments or empty or persuasive words 2Cor 11:3 Eph 5:6

desire beauty Prov 30:31

receive flattery and smooth words Rom 16:18 Prov 20:19

deceive ourselves James 1:22, 26 Gal 6:3 Jer 37:9 1Cor 3:18

allow other people to deceive us Mark 13:5, 6 Matt 24:4

listen to false prophets and false messiahs Matt 24:5, 11, 24 Jer 29:8; 14:14

worship false gods Deut 11:16 Isaiah 44:19d, 20

are not born again Jer 17:9, 10

trust the Men at Peace With Us Obad 7

Receive Honour from Men and do not seek the honour from God John 5:41, 44

Practise sinning Matt 7:21–23 1John 3:10

harbour Fierce Anger Jer 49:16a

pursue righteousness with God by our Works Gal 3:1 Col 2:16–23

forbid marriage and certain foods 1Tim 4:1–3

are covetous 2Pet 2:3

abide in every new doctrine and trickery of men Eph 4:14, 15

abide in the traditions of men Col 2:8

abide in the Counsels of the wicked Prov 12:5, 20

abide in the latest conspiracy theories: 2Thess 2:3 Neh 6:6

practice being Foolish Rom 1:21

commit to bad company and misplace our love and loyalty 1Cor 15:33 2Chron 19:2

practice indulging in harlotry, wine and new wine Hos 4:11, 12

do not know the scriptures or the power of God Mark 12:24–27

are corrupt, evil or are an imposter 2Tim 3:6–8; 13

practice laziness and inactivity James 1:22; 4:17

trust in the preacher only Acts 17:11

trust in our own ability to discern if somebody is lying Prov 18:17

trust in our own way Hos 10:13

practice sorcery and witchcraft Rev 18:23

CONCLUSION

We can be deceived if we trust in anything apart from the Lord. The wise trust in God and not men. Fundamentally we need to learn to trust in the Lord and to be prudent in our choices of which people to trust: Jer 17:5,7 "Cursed is the man who trusts in man and makes flesh his strength, whose heart departs from the Lord." ... 7 "Blessed is the man who trusts in the Lord, and whose hope is the Lord."

FURTHER TIPS TO GROW IN WISDOM

Col 2:2b,3 both of the Father and of Christ, 3 in whom are hidden all the treasures of wisdom and knowledge.

We can decide today to grow in wisdom, to work hard; to turn away from evil, to be prudent in how we live and commit ourselves to God's purposes in the church (Prov 4:18,19).

Godly wisdom is not meditating up on a mountain top, thinking erudite thoughts that nobody else can comprehend, the pursuit of philosophy and a higher knowledge, looking down upon others less educated, or talking slowly and meaningfully. All these have the appearance of wisdom. But such 'wisdom' can be a veil for deceit and partiality, which Job exposes in his friends in: Job 6:15 "My brothers have dealt deceitfully like a brook, like the streams of the brooks that pass away".

A wise person seeks God's will, advice and direction. Wisdom avoids problems and pitfalls, is spiritual in origin and comes from God. Col 1:9, 10 we do not cease to pray for you, and to ask that you may be filled with the knowledge of His will in all wisdom and spiritual understanding that you may walk worthy of the Lord ...

Wisdom will help us to be a success: Eccl 10:10
Wisdom assists in the effective use of time and speaks graciously: Col 4:5, 6; Eph 5:15–17

Wisdom brings happiness and joy: Prov 3:13, 14

We need to keep asking God for wisdom each day: James 1:5; Prov 2:6,7; Matt 7:7

Wisdom in speaking comfort: Isaiah 40:1–2; Prov 25:11; Rom 12:15

God teaches us wisdom and sensitivity in discipleship: Isaiah 28:23–29; Eccl 8:5

God relates to us with wisdom: Psalm 107

Recognise that the wise and prudent can become foolish: Isaiah 29:13,14

Recognise that people can be wise to do evil: Jer 4:22; 9:23,24; 1Cor 1:8–31

Spirit led decision making: Rom 8:14

Wisdom can be imparted: Deut 34:9; 1Tim 4:14; 2Tim 1:6

Wisdom asks for and receives advice: Prov 15:22; Prov 11:14; 13:10; 20:18

The wise are teachable and correctable: Prov 15:5,12,31,32; 19:20

A wise man rejects man's approval and discerns attempts to charm: Eccl 7:5; Prov 12:15; 24:23

Slow to anger indicates a greater understanding: Prov 14:29

Wisdom knows if and when to correct a fool: Prov 17:10; Eccl 7:5

Integrity: alignment of our values and principles with our church leadership: 2Cor 12:18

Wise men turn away wrath and do not vent their anger: Prov 29:8,11; 16:32; 19:11; 15:1; Eccl 7:9

Wisdom is quiet and listens but fools talk too much: Prov 14:33

Wise people seek God for greater revelation and understanding: Prov 25:2; Deut 29:29

Do not break confidentiality! Prov 25:9,10

The wise speak words in season: Prov 25:11,12; Eccl 8:5,6; 10:12

The wise mourn with those who mourn: Rom 12:15; Prov 25:20; Eccl 7:4

The wise recognise that there is a spiritual battle: 1Thess 2:18; Eph 4:27; 2Cor 2:10b,11

Wisdom hears both sides of the story and does not believe everything: Prov 14:15; Prov 18:13;17; 26:24,25

A wise man pays his vows on time and does not promise what he cannot deliver: Jam 5:12; Eccl 5:4,5; Ps 50:14; 56:12; 66:13; 76:11; Prov 20:25

The wise are of few words: Eccl 5:2,3; Prov 15:2

Wisdom does not long for "the good ol' days": Eccl 7:10

The wise do not vent their feelings and are not impulsive: Prov 10:19; 29:11; 29:20

A wise man does not flatter others and does not praise himself: Prov 26:28b; 27:2

We are tested when people praise us or when they criticize us: Prov 27:21

The wise leader promotes faithful, loyal people: Phil 2:22; 2Cor 8:22; 2Tim 2:2; 1Tim 3:10

The wise grow in wisdom and in discerning who to trust: Prov 11:13; 20:6

If we trust in our own heart we could make foolish decisions: Prov 28:26; Rom 8:14

The wise are humble and the proud are not wise: Prov 3:7; 16:5; 26:12; Jam 4:6

Be wise, watchful and prudent with the desire to be rich: Luke 12:15,34; 1Tim 6:8–10; Eccl 5:10; Prov 16:16

A fool and his money are soon parted: Prov 21:20

A wise person is unafraid of rejection from fools: Prov 13:14; 29:25,27; Deut 32:29

Acknowledgements

I would like to thank the Lord first and foremost as He is always our best comforter and encourager – His love and guidance have made all the difficulties of ministry worthwhile.

I would like to acknowledge my dear wife, Helen, who has been such a wonderful constant support over 30 years of ministry.

My HIM leaders, Ps Wilson and Ps Simon have been a huge blessing of strength and stability over the last 32 years of being in HIM together.

I would also like to thank those who read the manuscript and gave some constructive feedback and comments – especially those friends listed in the front of this book.

I also want to thank Ps Mapya (Democratic Republic of Congo, Central Africa), Ps Sonny (Liberia, West Africa) and Ps Ravi (India) whose example and commitment to the Great Commission have been inspiring over the last 12 to 17 years!

Eccl 7: 8 The end of a thing is better than its beginning; the patient in spirit is better than the proud in spirit.

Printed in the United States
by Baker & Taylor Publisher Services